VLADIMIR NABOKOV

Modern Literature Monographs

VLADIMIR NABOKOV

Donald E. Morton

Frederick Ungar Publishing Co.
New York

For Karen, Samantha, and our own
Humbert Humbert

Contents

Chronology

	two books of poetry containing more than 160 poems, only two or three of which are in English.
1925:	Marries Véra Evseevna Slonim.
1926:	*Mashenka* (novel) is published in Berlin.
1928:	*Korol', dama, valet* (novel) is published in Berlin.
1930:	*Zashchita Luzhina* and *Soglyadatay* (novels) are published in Berlin.
1932:	*Podvig* (novel), often referred to as *The Exploit*, is published in Paris. *Kamera obskura* (novel) is published in Paris and Berlin.
1934:	A son, Dmitri, is born in Berlin.
1935–36:	*Dar* (novel) is published partially in Paris; published in complete form in New York, 1952.
1936:	*Otchatyanie* (novel) is published in Berlin. *Camera obscura* (translation of the Russian novel by the same name) is published in London.
1937–40:	Lives in Paris.
1938:	*Priglashenie na kazn'* (novel) is published in Paris and Berlin. *Laughter in the Dark* (revised translation of *Kamera obskura*) is published. *Izobretenie Val'sa* (drama) is published in the émigré Russian journal *Russkie Zapiski*, in Paris.
1940:	The first part of *Solus Rex* (unfinished Russian novel) is published in *Contemporary Annals*, an émigré Russian journal, in Paris. May: Emigrates with wife and son to America.
1941:	*The Real Life of Sebastian Knight* (first novel written in English) is published.
1941–48:	Teaches at Wellesley College.
1942:	The second part of *Solus Rex* appears in Paris, under the title "Ultima Thule," in *The New Review*, an émigré Russian journal.
1942–48:	Works also in lepidopterology as a Fellow of the

Museum of Comparative Zoology, Harvard University.

1944:   *Nikolai Gogol* (critical biography) is published.

1945:   Becomes an American citizen.

1947:   *Bend Sinister* (novel) and *Nine Stories* (short stories) are published.

1948–59:   Holds professorship at Cornell University.

1951–52:   Lectures as guest at Harvard University.

1955:   *Lolita* (novel) is published in Paris.

1957:   *Pnin* (novel) is published.

1958:   *Nabokov's Dozen* (short stories) and *Lolita* are published in New York.

1959:   Moves to Montreux, Switzerland. *Invitation to a Beheading* (translation of *Priglashenie na kazn'*) and *Poems* are published.

1962:   *Pale Fire* (novel) is published.

1963:   *The Gift* (translation of *Dar*) is published.

1964:   Publishes monumental (and controversial) four-volume edition of Pushkin's *Eugene Onegin. The Defense* (translation of *Zashchita Luzhina*) is published.

1965:   *The Eye* (translation of *Soglyadatay*) is published.

1966:   *Speak, Memory* (memoir of the years 1903–1940) is published. An earlier version, called *Conclusive Evidence*, had been published in 1951. *Quartet* (short stories), *Despair* (translation of *Otchatyanie*), and *The Waltz Invention* (translation of *Izobretenie Val'sa*) are published.

1968:   *King, Queen, Knave* (translation of *Korol', dama, valet*) is published.

1969:   *Ada* (novel) is published.

1970:   *Poems and Problems*, consisting of thirty-nine Russian poems, with translations, fourteen Eng-

lish poems, eighteen chess problems, with solu-
tions, and a bibliography, is published. *Mary*
(translation of *Mashenka*) is published.

1971:   *Glory* (translation of *Podvig*) is published.

1972:   *Transparent Things* (novel) is published.

1973:   *A Russian Beauty, and Other Stories* (short
stories) is published. *Strong Opinions* (a collection of Nabokov's articles, letters, and opinions)
is published.

Introduction

Vladimir Nabokov's reputation in the English-speaking world is assured. Clarence Brown has referred to him as "the living master of English prose"; and, as if hinting to the selection committee, John Leonard has called him "The Nobel-est writer of them all."[1] Still more impressive than these individual appraisals is the result of a poll conducted a few years ago to determine the most distinguished contributors to American fiction in the postwar years, 1945–65. There Nabokov ranked high among the best-known novelists in America, among whom are also William Faulkner, Ernest Hemingway, Bernard Malamud, J. D. Salinger, Ralph Ellison, Norman Mailer, and Saul Bellow.[2]

In a 1967 interview, Nabokov seemed to minimize his personal success: "*Lolita* is famous, not I. I am an obscure, doubly obscure novelist with an unpronounceable name."[3] Even here the reader familiar with Nabokov's fiction sees the master's touch. Into a seemingly casual remark he has condensed a fine poignancy—and with characteristic playfulness. It was only after many years of creative struggle that fame came to him with the publication of his twelfth novel. At that, the struggle was necessarily carried out in several countries (Russia, Germany, France, and the United States) and in two languages: first Russian, then English.

Deprived through the fortunes of wars and revolutions of both his homeland and his language, Nabokov has brought to American fiction qualities not found to the same degree in the works of any other living writer. The nostalgia of his work is a persistent reminder that the world of his youth, not actually so distant in time, is lost to him, except in memory. Still the richness of that heritage lingers about all he has written and gives shape and substance even to a novel like *Lolita*, ostensibly devoted to American life. While he has asserted that he is "as

American as April in Arizona," the remark is more poetry than fact.[4]

On the contrary, Nabokov's ties with America do not bind him tightly. When the success of *Lolita* gave him financial independence, Nabokov and his wife moved to Switzerland. What he seems to cherish most about America are just those things that remind him of the past. "The flora and the fauna, the air of the Western states" are his "links with Asiatic and Arctic Russia."[5] Separated by necessity from his native country, never fully assimilated into his adopted one, Nabokov has made his real home in the worlds of the imagination.

Nabokov takes impish pleasure in the difficulty his career presents to literary historians and critics. "Nobody can decide," he has said, "if I am a middle-aged American writer or an old Russian writer—or an ageless international freak."[6] For him the literary historian's embarrassment is one of the best signs that he has achieved the high standards he has set for himself. The mystifying nature of his career reflects the uniqueness he prizes most in an artist. Everything he has written goes to support his idea, expressed in *Pnin*, that "genius is nonconformity." His own conception of the artistic process minimizes practically to zero the role played by external influences, such as what the writer has read, whom he has known, and what historical or even personal events take place while he is working, and maximizes to the greatest possible extent the role played by genius.

With his usual candor, Nabokov has recently expressed his nonconformity in literary matters. Aware that his remarks sounded old-fashioned in a time when literary theory is more complicated and ambitious than ever, Nabokov announced in January 1973 his belief in the simple-sounding idea that artistic creativity is a matter of inspiration.[7]

What he stresses in such statements and everywhere in his creative work is the subjective nature of art. This subjectivity is complex. At times Nabokov expresses his understanding of it by calling attention to the importance of the artist's mastery of his materials. Asked once what he thought of E. M. Forster's well-known notion that characters in fiction occasionally grow so vital as to break free of their creator and follow their own wishes, Nabokov defended the idea of tyrannical control. "My characters," he replied, "are galley slaves."[8] Craftsmanship and artistic control are for him supreme virtues.

Yet the issue is not so simple, for Nabokov does believe that the work of art has a life of its own, though his way of expressing the notion is different from Forster's. Behind the artist's conscious control, behind his deliberate selection of words and phrases, themes and motifs, lies a more mysterious subjective process. Nabokov has spoken also about this dimension of art:

I am afraid to get mixed up with Plato whom I do not care for, but I do think that in my case it is true that the entire book, before it is written, seems to be ready ideally in some other, now transparent, now dimming, dimension, and my job is to take down as much of it as I can make out and as precisely as I am humanly able to. The greatest happiness I experience in composition is when I feel I cannot understand, or rather catch myself not understanding (without the presupposition of an already existing creation) how or why that image or structural move has come to me.[9]

Thus, paradoxically, the artist is on the one hand a demigod, fashioning the world of his fiction according to his own lights, and on the other a recording mechanism, whose function is a strangely passive, almost secretarial one.

It is the idealistic spirit of these remarks about genius, inspiration, and the creative process that one must come to understand before fully appreciating Nabokov's fiction, for his work consistently challenges many common conceptions of the relation between life and art, ethics and aesthetics. If one can generalize as far as to say that fiction falls into the two broad categories of realism and romance, Nabokov's work belongs in the latter category. The reader of today is likely to find the romance of Nabokov's art strangely archaic and old-fashioned. In some ways he seems to have stronger affinities with the nineteenth century than with the twentieth. This affinity is not simply an accident of age and environment, of the fact that he was born at the turn of the century in Saint Petersburg, the cultural center of nineteenth-century Russia, but a matter of temperament and conscious choice. Nabokov himself has named Poe, Melville, Hawthorne, and Emerson as "the great American writers" he most admires.[10] Not only does the list seem strangely dated for a man still active as a writer in the 1970s, it is also categorically selective. The writers he named are the classic figures of the American romantic period.

Nabokov shows a similar affinity with the romantic writers of Russian literature. In 1964 he published a four-volume translation of and commentary on *Eugene Onegin*, a novel in verse by Alexander Pushkin (1799–1837), who was early in his career a disciple of the English romantic poet, Lord Byron.[11] Nabokov has claimed that there is nothing unusual in his interest in Pushkin, since—as he has said—Pushkin is to Russian literature what Shakespeare is to English. Nevertheless, the connection is closer and more significant than Nabokov's demur suggests. After surveying the evidence for the influence of the older writer on Nabokov, one critic gave the question this pointed summation: "Pushkin is Nabokov's fate."[12]

Though extreme, the remark illuminates the center of Nabokov's art. What he achieves in his fiction is a compelling fusion of past and present, fancy and fact, poetry and prose, romance and his own special brand of realism.

Not only does Nabokov's work seem to have closer affinities with the literary traditions of the nineteenth century than with those of the twentieth, but his fiction often seems to have greater affinities with poetry, especially romantic poetry, than with the novel, as it is usually thought of. W. H. Auden's discussion of romanticism is helpful in understanding Nabokov's ties to that movement. Each age, according to Auden, has a spiritual and artistic unity, a world view that is reflected in its literature and in the image of man evoked by that literature. As opposed to the medieval poet, who celebrated moral will, or the eighteenth-century poet, who celebrated reason, the romantic poet—according to Auden—held that man's most important faculty is consciousness itself. The function of consciousness, he says, is to register and record impressions, both internal and external. Unlike moral will, however, consciousness cannot in and of itself alone distinguish good from evil. Unlike reason, it cannot distinguish the true from the false. All consciousness can do is record its impulses along a scale of intensity.

Through his commitment to consciousness, the romantic poet has naturally diminished the importance of moral and empirical judgments. For this poet, morality remains at best a secondary interest, a social convention. For him also, the dream is as compelling as external reality. Moreover, since his own consciousness is the only one he really knows, it becomes his most important subject.[13]

Auden's description of the romantic poet fits Nabokov with surprising exactness. First, the opening pages of Nabokov's autobiography, *Speak, Memory,* are nothing

less than a hymn of praise to the powers of human consciousness. Life, he says there, is a series of "extraordinary visions" between "the two black voids" of those mysterious periods before one's birth and after one's death.
As long as one is alive, consciousness is all-powerful and
all-embracing: "How small the cosmos (a kangaroo's
pouch would hold it), how paltry and puny in comparison
to human consciousness, to a single individual recollec-
tion, and its expression in words!"

With the dawning of consciousness, one is enabled
—especially in the freshness of childhood—to "feed upon
beauty" and "hoard up impressions." The process is particularly acute for the sensitive child, since his mind
becomes charged with impressions, whose weight creates
the need for artistic expression. Nabokov says that as a
child he "slipped" his hoarded-up impressions "into a
pocket of black velvet," that is, into his consciousness,
where they lay like a treasure: "diamonds that I later
gave away to my characters to alleviate the burden of
my wealth."

Second, since in Nabokov's view the creative process
is a cycle of charging consciousness with highly particu-
larized and personal impressions and then of discharging
those impressions into words, he can be only tangentially
interested in questions of morality and social realism. On
many occasions, Nabokov has affirmed his total lack of
interest in literature that aims at teaching a moral lesson.
Probably the best-known such occasion is the passage in
the postscript to *Lolita* in which he asserts that he is
"neither a reader nor a writer of didactic fiction." In this
connection, one should keep in mind the moral controversy surrounding the publication of *Lolita*. A number of
American publishers declined to accept the manuscript,
since it dealt with the love affair of a middle-aged man

and a twelve-year-old girl, before Maurice Girodias of the Olympia Press finally published it in Paris in 1955.

As for the question of the need for realism in the novel, Nabokov has dismissed the idea of "everyday reality" as itself a fiction.[14] Since for Nabokov individual perception constitutes reality, there are as many realities as individuals. Therefore art cannot be a reflection of a common reality.

Lastly, though his works are remarkably varied (he has written not only novels and an autobiography, but also biography, translations, literary criticism, drama, short stories, and poetry), the voice speaking in these many genres is recognizably the same. Nabokov's audacious style, which calls attention as much to itself as to what it is meant to convey, leaves its mark on all he writes. In other words, like Auden's romantic poet, Nabokov is always his own most important subject.

Nabokov is a self-affirmed agnostic in matters religious, political, and philosophical. The best-known ideologies of the Western world (Freudian psychology, in particular) have been at one time or another the objects of his scorn. In his view, "mediocrity thrives on 'ideas.' "[15] This does not mean, however, that he would replace these ideologies with one he thinks is better; only that the strongest imperative for him is the preservation of his artistic and intellectual freedom.

As the foregoing discussion suggests, Nabokov is also something of an agnostic when it comes to questions of art. He has said little about literary creativity except that it depends on the artist's having a highly developed consciousness (by which word he means the recording mechanism of perception, the function of memory, and the powers of selection and combination; that is, the powers of the imagination as they operate under the guidance of inspiration) and a mastery of language. In his own practice the stress is on describing human experience —*as he has known it*—with the greatest degree of articulation and the finest discrimination possible, rather than on judging it.

Uninterested in didacticism or in realism, Nabokov is committed only to the purity of aesthetic experience, to the joys of what he has called, again in the postscript to *Lolita*, "aesthetic bliss." His talent is to conjure up for his readers the kind of bliss he has experienced in his own life: thinking of a person he loves, enjoying the fine strokes of a tennis player, constructing a sublime chess problem, discovering a species of butterfly never known before. The pleasure in these moments of aesthetic bliss arises from the conscious savoring of details, of colors, textures, patterns, designs.

These still points of ecstasy come, Nabokov says in *Speak, Memory*, not in dreams, "but when one is wide awake, at moments of robust joy and achievement, on the highest terrace of consciousness." It is then "that mortality has a chance to peer beyond its own limits, from the mast, from the past and its castle tower." In other words, the conscious savoring of beauty is the nearest approach man ever makes to understanding the larger questions with which ideologies usually deal, such as the meaning of life and death, and the existence of God. Nabokov, however, is the first to admit that these moments of aesthetic bliss offer one only a glimpse in the direction of the answers to those great questions: " . . . although nothing much can be seen through the mist, there is somehow the blissful feeling that one is looking in the right direction."

Nabokov's work is marked by two equally strong propensities: the reluctance to judge and the passion to describe. In a man of his talent, the former makes him a great ironist; the latter makes him a great stylist. For the reader, these virtues also constitute his limitations. Because his works are formed of layers upon layers of irony (expressed in what he himself has referred to as a "Rolls Royce" prose), they do not make for easy reading. The quantity of irony means that the reader's willingness to suspend his judgment of characters and their actions is taxed to the limit. As soon as the reader thinks he has found the basis for judging a character or an action, that basis suddenly disappears in a typical Nabokovian flourish of ironic magic.

Nabokov has a decided preference for protagonists who are either geniuses or madmen, and sometimes both. His favorite characters are socially marginal types, and it is their very eccentricity—their special sensitivity, their special powers of perceptivity or creativity—that makes them to his mind appropriate artistic subjects. That their eccentricity also tends to exempt them from moral judgment creates a problem for the reader inclined to seek moral significance in fiction.

The majority of Nabokov's readers will always wish to know what bearing his fables have on life as they know it. Many may wonder, as Joyce Carol Oates recently did, why Nabokov "assigns worth . . . quite exaggerated, even ludicrous . . . to a few selected human beings, focusing his imagination on the happy few, lavishing contempt and energetic humor upon most other people."[16] Though Miss Oates was speaking here primarily about *Ada*, she apparently sees that work as representative of Nabokov's entire canon and her criticism as appropriate to Nabokov's artistic practice in general. Most immediately one may answer this sensible-sounding, but I think unjust, question by pointing out that Nabokov's characters cannot be called "happy" in any ordinary sense of that word. (This is true, by the way, even of the protagonists of *Ada*, for whom Navokov obviously has a special affection.) Nabokov's characters suffer much too much to be called "the happy few."

The more important question is why his characters are *not* happy in the conventional sense. It is most certainly because they possess a purely Nabokovian worthiness and happiness: their worthiness consists, as one might expect, in their powers of consciousness, and their happiness, in their moments of aesthetic bliss. This bliss is a state of ecstasy, which means in its original sense, *ex-stasis*, or standing outside of oneself.

Further, to understand the necessity of their suffering, one need only reflect for a moment on Auden's ideas, and extend one of them to its logical conclusion. Unable to distinguish good from evil or right from wrong, all consciousness can do, he says, is record its impressions along a scale of intensity. It is generally known that at a certain level of intensity what begins as pleasure may turn into pain. Nabokov's typical protagonist is both blessed and victimized by a kind of holy madness, a power that is both a gift and a burden.

The stress of subjectivity makes Nabokov and his characters (who, as a number of critics have pointed out, are all "little Nabokovs") sound like solipsists, like individuals completely wrapped up in their own mental worlds. It is as if they have no sense whatever of the objective existence of an outer reality. While this is true in part, it would be misleading to leave the matter there, for even they are aware that consciousness receives its impressions from an outer world. Though Auden's romantic poet may prefer the dream world to the world of waking reality, Nabokov does not; the perceptions he receives in the state of wakeful consciousness are what he prizes most. In *Speak, Memory* he goes so far as to say that "sleep is the most moronic fraternity in the world, with the heaviest dues, and the crudest rituals . . . I simply cannot get used to the nightly betrayal of reason, humanity, genius. No matter how great my weariness, the wrench of parting with consciousness is unspeakably repulsive to me." For both Nabokov and his characters, the sensations they receive from the outer world are crucial.

The suffering of Nabokov's characters comes both from within and from without. Agnostics like their creator, sure of nothing but the steady flow of sensations, his characters are, in fact, desperately dependent on the external world. Through their passion for intensity they victimize themselves; and hence their suffering is in part self-created. Yet, at the same time, their suffering has a corresponding source in the external world. Not only is the world devilishly seductive and tantalizing, but also the impressions one receives from it seem at times to form themselves into significative patterns and designs, leading one to the momentary hope that the world holds a meaning of its own, an innate meaning not imparted to it by the perceiver. As these patterns form and dissolve, so the hope quickens and dwindles, leaving the perceiver with nothing but memories. The humanity of Nabokov's characters is based on no philosophical, political, or religious system, on no creed or ideology, but simply on the dignity with which they confront this mirage of hope.

This is surely a view of life born of Nabokov's personal experience. Having seen how fate plays games with man, leaving traces here and there, clues that hint at a whole design or pattern, at a coherent and rational meaning innate in the external world, Nabokov plays the part of fate in the world of his fiction. In the style and form of his fictional worlds, countless moments of aesthetic bliss are available to the reader willing to alter his habitual mode of perception, willing to take—if only temporarily— the aesthetic stance.

1

*Roots
of Remembered
Greenery*

Vladimir Vladimirovich Nabokov was born on 22 April 1899, into a distinguished and aristocratic family, just the kind that ceased to exist in the wake of the Russian Revolution. Saint Petersburg, the place of his birth, was at the time Russia's most westward-looking city. Surrounded by troops of servants, the Nabokovs divided their time between Saint Petersburg during the harsh winters and their country estate, Vyra, located fifty miles to the south during the summers. Along with his siblings (two boys, two girls, all younger than he), Nabokov enjoyed in childhood frequent excursions abroad, to Berlin, to Paris, and to resorts on the Riviera and the Adriatic. As he reveals in his memoir, *Speak, Memory*, those long days and nights on the train, with their endless succession of passing images, provided Nabokov with some of his sharpest early thrills and were a great stimulus to his power of "hoarding up impressions." His delight in railway travel once led him to name one of his mother's dogs "Trainy" (she had a fondness for Dachshunds), "because of his being as long and as brown as a sleeping car."

The picture that emerges from Nabokov's reminiscences is that of a liberal and Westernized family, whose talented members turned their vitality into many avenues of interest—politics, medicine, law, music, literature, science, sports—each member usually into more than one. His youthful environment has for the contemporary American a strangely Victorian air. In that archaic, genteel life style, the gentleman-scholar mixing scientific and artistic researches was the norm rather than the exception. Into this pattern, Nabokov, with his passions for etymology and entomology (to be specific, lepidopterology), for words and butterflies, easily fit.

Though he spent his youth in the twilight of the feudal past, a twilight that came later in Russia than in the countries of Western Europe, Nabokov reserves a special resentment for those who, particularly under the influence of the sham democratic slogans of communism, tend to think of him and his family as living in a luxury bought with the oppression of the poor. While making no excuses for the privileges he enjoyed, he insists that what he regrets losing most is not the millions he stood to inherit, but the natural treasures, the flora and fauna of the motherland, and especially the riches of the intellectual and cultural milieu in which he was nurtured. There were, of course, enormous differences of class and rank in his Russia; but the intelligentsia of which his father was a member by choice, Nabokov says was "classless."

In Nabokov's view of Russian history, the Bolshevik Revolution was an obvious tragedy, since it destroyed all possibility of genuine culture by forcing human beings to measure their experiences in terms of the lowest common denominator. But for him an extra poignancy was added by the fact that his father, Vladimir Dmitrievich Nabokov, worked during the first two decades of the twentieth century as a member of the hopeful movement to thwart the despotic policies of the tsar and to democratize Russian politics. Vladimir senior was a lover of literature, a prolific writer on political and legal subjects (he was a jurist by training), and after the revolution editor of the liberal émigré newspaper, *The Rudder*, a Russian-language daily published in Berlin. In 1922, while Nabokov was studying at Cambridge, his father was mistakenly killed at a political rally in Berlin by an assassin whose bullet was intended for the speaker whom Vladimir Dmitrievich was there to introduce.

His father's guidance was particularly strong in matters of education. He insisted on a variety of tutors for his children in order to expose them to different races, nationalities, and languages. The family's Anglophilia

(Nabokov says in *Speak, Memory* that his father was "an authority on Dickens") was so pronounced that at the age of six, Navokov could read and write English but not Russian. Countless details in Nabokov's fiction are drawn from his father's interests and opinions and even from events in his life. On the personal side, Nabokov has said, their relationship "was marked by that habitual exchange of homespun nonsense, comically garbled words, proposed imitations of supposed intonations, and all those private jokes which is the secret code of happy families." Nabokov tells in *Speak, Memory* some touching reminiscences of his father; especially affecting are those concerned with their common passion for butterfly-hunting, the drama of a duel his father once fought, and the painful moment when the family fled Bolshevik-controlled Saint Petersburg for the temporary safety of the Crimea, leaving father Nabokov behind.

While the relationship with his father was close, Navokov had an equally strong temperamental affinity with his mother. As a child Nabokov displayed an unusual aptitude for mathematics and a gift for synesthetic response—that is, visual stimuli sometimes triggered in him auditory responses and vice versa. These abilities were often strongest during his bouts with childhood illnesses. The mathematical precocity faded early, but his mother did everything she could to encourage her son's sensitivity, especially his visual sensitivity. An amateur painter herself, she enlisted the aid of her own former tutor for enriching Nabokov's already lively response to colors. Later he was succeeded by another tutor, one of whose favorite exercises was to have his young charge sketch from memory objects whose very familiarity made the recall of details a challenge even for an intelligent and observant child.

Such exercises doubtless helped to shape the vividness and precision of the richly descriptive prose Nabokov was later to develop. Nabokov shared two other prominent qualities of his mother. One was an abiding love of nature, which she expressed in many ways, most memorably, perhaps, by her frequent excursions into the woods around Vyra to search for edible mushrooms. The other was the belief in the value of passionate intensity. In *Speak, Memory* Nabokov refers to one of her favorite maxims: "To love with all one's soul and leave the rest to fate, was the simple rule she heeded."

Fate's powerful place in Nabokov's fiction can be accounted for in two major ways. One is literary; the other, biographical. R. H. W. Dillard has stated the case from the literary side: "The Russian novel is traditionally the product of Russian fatalism; the world of Russian literature is one in which a coincidence is a controlled event and in which the creative freedom of man is involved in the discovery of the pattern of his destiny rather than forming that future himself out of the chaos of possibilities."[1] Fate's harsh handling of Nabokov's own life could only have seemed to reinforce such a view. In his last years in Russia, Nabokov lived with an inner and an outer turbulence. His first love affair, initially a summer, country idyll and then a more desperate search in wintry Saint Petersburg for a spot where the lovers could be alone, dwindled into an "incomprehensible separation," while Nabokov indulged in the sensual experiments that he thought requisite for an aspiring poet. At about the same time, in 1916, he published his first book of verse, which prompted one of his cousins, himself a famous poet, to plead that Nabokov "never, never be a writer."

Matching these natural pangs of adolescence, all the more anguishing for a sensitive youth, were the political upheavals. At the end of 1917, when Lenin took power,

Nabokov's father sent the entire family to the Crimea. They were, as Nabokov says, "absolutely ruined," except for a few jewels thoughtfully stashed away against future need. After some months they were joined by their father, and they departed, in May 1919, for a life of exile in the West.

As he has described them, Nabokov's years at Trinity College, Cambridge, were unsettling. People tended to respond to him as an interesting foreigner and as a type, a "White Russian." Political conversations frequently turned out badly. He found himself caught between those who patronizingly "understood" his situation, without understanding it at all; those socialists who were sympathetic to the new regime in his homeland; and other Russian émigré students who seemed only concerned with the loss of their wealth. Reacting in fear of assimilation and the total loss of the past he had known, Nabokov concentrated on Russian literature and language, paying little heed to his new surroundings (except for the soccer field, the tennis courts, and girls). Not once, according to him, did he visit the university library.

The death of his father in March 1922 brought several changes. After the funeral, he returned for his last term with the determination to do well and took his degree with honors in Russian and French literature. His brother Sergey had a similar success at the same time at Christ College. Within months of their new tragedy, the family dispersed. Nabokov's mother moved the following year to Prague with the three younger children, while Sergey went to Paris and Vladimir remained in Berlin, to which he had returned after graduation. There he wrote a good deal of verse, much of which was published, "unripe" according to him, in Russian émigré papers. He supported himself by tutoring German youths and businessmen in English, by coaching tennis, and even (as he revealed only recently in an interview) by appearing as "a tuxedoed extra" in German films.[2]

By 1926 Véra Evseevna Slonim was Nabokov's wife, and his first novel, *Mary*, had been published. For a little more than a decade thereafter, Nabokov continued to live in Berlin with Véra and their first and only child, Dmitri, born in 1934. There, in the circle of Russian exiles numbering perhaps 200,000 and centered primarily in the southwest suburbs of the German capital, Nabokov published eight novels under the pseudonym Vladimir Sirin, and acquired a reputation as a prose stylist.[3]

These years in Europe formed the first stage of Nabokov's life of exile. In *Speak, Memory*, he commented on fate's strange design for him: his life, he observed, seemed to unfold in approximately twenty-year segments. His first two decades (1899–1919) were spent in his native Russia; the next twenty-one years (1919–40), in Western Europe, primarily in the Russian communities in Berlin and Paris. He moved his family to Paris in 1937, where he published his last Russian-language novel; and from France they sailed to America in May 1940.

In the United States Nabokov found not only economic security but world-wide fame. He turned his several scholarly talents to advantage in academia. After a brief stay at Stanford in 1940, he taught Russian at Wellesley College from 1941–48, working simultaneously, from 1942–48, in lepidopterology as a Fellow of Harvard's Museum of Comparative Zoology. As early as 1938, two years before setting out for America, Nabokov had gone through the anguishing trial of discovering whether or not he could write as successfully in English as in Russian. In spite of his other interests and duties, he managed to begin his career as an English-language writer in his first decade in America, publishing *The Real Life of Sebastian Knight* in 1941 (though it had been written in

Paris in 1938), his critical study of Gogol in 1944, and *Bend Sinister* in 1947. That his remarkable talent was recognized early is evidenced by the awards he received; a grant from the Guggenheim Foundation (1943, and in 1953) and an award from the American Academy of Arts and Letters (also in 1953).

But the decade he spent as professor of literature at Cornell University (1948–59) brought the real beginnings of Nabokov's fame. There are published testimonies to his success as a teacher as well as a writer.[4] His classroom technique was apparently a combination of iconoclasm and dramatic reading. He enjoyed debunking not only some sacred intellectual gods, such as Freud, Marx, and Darwin, but literary ones as well. Ross Wetzsteon has reported that he, like most other students Nabokov taught in the early 1950s at Cornell, were unaware at the time that Nabokov was himself a writer.[5] Morris Bishop, one of Nabokov's colleagues at Cornell, has written about the stir *Lolita* might have caused among alumni and trustees had the American publication not been delayed until 1958, three years after the Paris edition had become an underground success.[6] By the time Nabokov left Cornell and teaching in 1959, the intervening success of *Lolita* had made him a celebrity and his course had a high enrollment.

The literary evaluation of so complex a work as *Lolita* is a challenging task, but it is relatively easy to assess its meaning for Nabokov's career as a writer. With its appearance, he was recognized as one of America's best writers of fiction. More important, his meteoric rise allowed for another remarkable achievement, the publication of twenty-five more books since 1958. His nine Russian novels have all by now appeared in English, along with a number of his short stories, and a fraction of his poems.

In 1960, Nabokov's life entered its fourth phase. While retaining their American citizenship, he and his wife moved in that year to Montreux, Switzerland, in part to be near their son, who is both an opera singer and a translator of his father's works, and in part perhaps to be nearer to their roots. There in the rented rooms on the sixth floor of the Montreux Palace Hotel, they continue their life of spiritual exile, but in comfort and international fame. Though he is claimed by America, and himself rejects completely the idea of ever returning to Russia (he once had invitations to do so), Nabokov still seems to think of himself as a Russian writer. When asked in 1970 why he had moved to Montreux, Nabokov replied, "It's fitting for a Russian writer to settle in this region —Tolstoy came here as a youth, Dostoevsky and Chekhov visited, and Gogol began *Dead Souls* nearby."[7]

Russian though he may be, Nabokov's conquest of America has already moved from literature into the other arts and is about to move even further. *Lolita* was made into a successful film some years ago, *King, Queen, Knave* has just been released, and *Ada* is going into production. What's more, Nabokov is branching out to Broadway, for Alan Lerner is preparing the lyrics for a musical version of *Lolita*.[8]

2

The Gloom and the Glory of Exile: The Russian Novels

While the bulk of the present study is devoted to the novels Nabokov wrote originally in English, behind this work there lies what was once the vast terra incognita of his Russian poems, plays, short stories, and novels. Though it came many years after he published his first English novel, the stature Nabokov achieved with the publication of *Lolita*, and even more with *Pale Fire*, finally permitted him to naturalize his Russian works, so to speak, by making them available to English-speaking readers. So, from the late 1950s through the early 1970s, he not only wrote and published a number of new works, but also translated or supervised the translation of eight of his nine Russian novels (*Camera obscura*, or as it was later called, *Laughter in the Dark*, had already been published in English in the 1930s, without receiving much notice). Once Nabokov had become famous, the translation of these works was inevitable.

Relatively few readers, critics, or historians (the present writer included) are competent in both languages and literatures; hence, the problems associated with the appreciation and assessment of Nabokov as a writer have been somewhat relieved by the translation of his older fiction. Yet these problems are far from being fully resolved. The situation is not the sort usually found in comparative literature. There an author from one linguistic and literary context is set against another from a quite different linguistic and literary context; and in such a case one typically commences by frankly assuming a wide latitude of unbridgeable differences.

Nabokov's case is significantly different. Here we have the same writer with two careers, one mind fashioning what must be in many essential ways a consistent vision, but a vision projected under the pressure of two distinct linguistic and literary traditions. Though Nabokov himself denies the importance of the dual nature of his career, the differences of language and culture have inescapable effects. One can clearly see these effects, for example, in the last of his Russian novels, *The Gift*. Nabokov himself has called it the best of his Russian novels, but even so knowledgeable an American reader as Granville Hicks has claimed that the novel is hard going, not so much because of the games the author plays, but because "it was written for an audience saturated with Russian literature."[1]

Even a scholar competent in both Russian and English, such as Andrew Field, whose work has laid the foundation for decades of future study, tends in his handling of the relation of Nabokov's two bodies of fiction to stop at drawing parallels of plot and characterization, without engaging in discussion of matters such as style, which depends so much on differences of language. Yet for Nabokov, style is all-important. While he has made it possible for those who do not know Russian to read his earlier novels, Nabokov has simultaneously created other difficulties by sometimes making the English versions significantly different from the originals (this is particularly true of *King, Queen, Knave, Despair,* and *Laughter in the Dark*).

Of necessity two bodies of criticism have formed around Nabokov's writings, that by Russian scholars and that by English and American ones. The gap between the two, a gap as yet only narrowly bridged, gives rise to peculiar critical predicaments. One illustration can be found in the contrasting views offered by the American critic, R. H. W. Dillard and by the distinguished Slavicist, Gleb Struve. Writing primarily of Nabokov's English fiction, Dillard stressed the "Russianness" of those novels, for he found in them a consistent focus on what he called "Russian fatalism."[2] Writing of Nabokov's émigré novels, Struve reported that Russian émigré critics them-

selves stressed the "un-Russianness" even of Nabokov's
Russian novels.[3] The contrast of these opinions hints at
the difficulties presented by Nabokov's mixed canon. Since
in addition to the problems already mentioned, a good
deal of his Russian writings has not yet been translated, it
seems best to keep one's eye on the core of works that
were originally written in English and to examine the
translated Russian works only as a background to these.
Nabokov has, after all, achieved his greatest success as
an English-language writer.

The nine Russian novels, written and published
between 1925 and 1940 mostly in Berlin, were primarily
responsible for Nabokov's being, again according to Gleb
Struve, "almost unanimously recognized as the most original and brilliant product of émigré literature."[4] In his
excellent book, *Nabokov, His Life in Art*, Andrew Field
describes Nabokov's uneasy rise in the ranks of the
émigré writers. According to Field, the first novel, *Mashenka* (*Mary*), was generally ignored; the second, *Korol',
dama, valet* (*King, Queen, Knave*), produced some interest. The third and fourth, *Zashchita Luzhina* (*The
Defense*) and *Soglyadatay* (*The Eye*), caused considerable discussion, not all of it favorable. The debate about
the novels of Nabokov (then using the name Sirin) continued as new ones appeared: *Podvig* (*Glory*), *Camera
obscura* (*Laughter in the Dark*), *Dar* (*The Gift*), *Otchatyanie* (*Despair*), and *Priglashenie na Kazn'* (*Invitation
to a Beheading*). Yet by the time the last had appeared,
in 1938, the Russian exiles in Berlin were feeling, like
many others, the pressure of the growing Nazi terrorism,
and the Nabokovs had moved to Paris.[5]

Without at all intending to denigrate Nabokov's talent, Clarence Brown once remarked that Nabokov's work
is "extremely repetitious." "For well over a quarter of a
century now," Brown wrote in 1967, Nabokov "has been

writing in book after book about the same thing."[6]
Brown's point is well taken, as I hope to show in the following pages. Though each new book by Nabokov seems
to have a different subject, there is in his total canon a
homogeneity of theme and technique. Nabokov himself
has agreed, with characteristic wit: "I do not think I have
seen Clarence Brown's essay," he told Herbert Gold in
an interview in 1967, "but he may have something there.
Derivative writers seem versatile because they imitate
many others, past and present. Artistic originality has
only its own self to copy."[7]

For all their apparent variety, there is a clearly
observable thematic unity in Nabokov's Russian novels,
just as there is in his English ones. *Mary, King, Queen,
Knave*, and *Laughter in the Dark* are loosely linked
together as love stories. *Mary* centers on the nostalgic
yearning of the protagonist, Lev Ganin, for the girl he has
left behind in Russia, the title character, who herself
never actually appears. At the novel's opening, Ganin, a
Russian émigré in Berlin, meets a fellow boarder at a
pension, Aleksey Alfyorov, in a stalled elevator. Alfyorov
is anticipating the arrival in six days of his wife, whom
he has not seen in four years but who has been allowed to
leave the Soviet Union to join him. Much of the novel is
devoted to detailing the varied lives of the other émigré
boarders in the *pension*; but halfway through it, Ganin
realizes that the wife Alfyorov is so happily awaiting is
in fact Mary, the girl he has always loved. Though he successfully plots to get Alfyorov drunk and make him late
for Mary's train so that he himself can meet her, Ganin
realizes that she will not be the same woman he once
knew, and leaves the station before encountering her.

The details of the novel amply reflect the conditions
of émigré life in Berlin, and the absent girl is a symbol
of the exiles' longing for their lost homeland. It is a novel

about the dangers of nostalgia, which—as Nabokov says in his introduction to the work—tends to remain "throughout one's life an insane companion."

Nabokov was stimulated to write *King, Queen, Knave* by reading a Russian translation of a tale with the same title by Hans Christian Andersen. There is little or no resemblance between the two works in terms of content, Andersen's tale being about a palace revolt and Nabokov's about a love triangle, the principal characters all belonging obviously to the hearts suit. Andrew Field and Charles Nicol have observed that the connection between the two works is one of technique.[8] Nabokov was evidently fascinated by the cardlike two-dimensionality of Andersen's characters, and he utilized the card metaphor even to the extent of matching the number of the novel's chapters to the number of cards in a suit—thirteen. One might add to Field's and Nicol's observations the fact that the novel was written only half a dozen years after Nabokov, as a student at Cambridge, had translated Lewis Carroll's *Alice in Wonderland* into Russian. The strange, blank objectivity with which Nabokov handles his characters reflects the weird anthropomorphizing of inanimate objects (cards, among other things) that takes place in the Wonderland world.

The principal characters—the novel's first readers found them alien since they are German rather than Russian—are Franz, a provincial lad who comes to Berlin and finds a job in a department store; his uncle, Dreyer, a businessman and the owner of the store, and Dreyer's wife, Martha. Bored with her moody husband, Martha seduces the nephew and enlists his help in a plan to murder Dreyer. When the plan is delayed, Martha becomes ill and dies before it can be reactivated, leaving the sad husband with more love for her than he thought he possessed and young Franz, who had become her reluctant tool, relieved that the murder had never taken place. In his foreword to the English translation, Nabokov has referred to the novel as a "gay," "bright brute," and his handling of the characters does indeed suggest the kind of detachment he later displayed toward the sufferings of his better-known heroes and heroines.

In *Laughter in the Dark* Nabokov reexplored the fictional possibilities of a love triangle, but with a highly sophisticated permutation. By the pervasive use of cinematic analogies, he grounded the fantasy world of his third novel in a film motif.[9] Though this motif was apparently more overt in the original Russian novel, Dabney Stuart has recently demonstrated that it is one of the principal thematic and structural features of the considerably altered English version.[10]

Laughter in the Dark opens with a concise summary of its fable:

Once upon a time there lived in Berlin, Germany, a man called Albinus. He was rich, respectable, happy; one day he abandoned his wife for the sake of a youthful mistress; he loved; was not loved; and his life ended in disaster.

As the opening lines suggest, the novel records the tragedy of a man who is blinded by love; but what it does not reveal is that Albinus Kretschmar's metaphorical blindness is made concrete when he is literally blinded in an accident. The young woman he loves, Margot Peters, meets him when she is working as an usherette in a movie theater. She deliberately attracts the rich Kretschmar in order to use him to subsidize the career in films that she has always dreamed of having. After Kretschmar's blindness, his mistress betrays him by renewing her affair with the cartoonist, Axel Rex. Kretschmar's initial vulnerability is then painfully exaggerated by one of those bizarre touches for which Nabokov is famous. Axel Rex moves in with Margot and blind Albinus, without the latter's knowledge. Albinus is thus shadowed daily by a man who cuckolds him, the pantomiming Axel. Albinus's murder at the novel's end is a miniature anticipation of Humbert Humbert's stage-directed murder of Clare Quilty, which comes twenty years later in *Lolita*.

Although the most obvious connection between *Mary, King, Queen, Knave*, and *Laughter in the Dark* is that provided by the theme of love, there is in them a much more significant theme relating them not only to Nabokov's other Russian novels, but to his English novels as well. Albinus Kretschmar's blindness only makes overt what was latent in the two earlier novels: the theme of perception. In *Mary*, Ganin and Alfyorov meet when, in the "unexpected darkness" of a stalled elevator, they decide to introduce themselves. Quite pointedly, Alfyorov asks Ganin:

"Don't you think there's something symbolic in our meeting like this . . . the fact that we've stopped, motionless, in this darkness. And that we're waiting. At lunch today that man— what's his name—the old writer—oh, yes, Podtyagin—was arguing with me about the sense of this émigré life of ours, this perpetual waiting."

Through the implications of Alfyorov's statement, Nabokov suggests the blindness of the émigrés' way of life. Essentially oblivious to their surroundings in Berlin, they dwell within their memories of the Russia they left behind. Nabokov reinforces the message, oddly enough, by making the happiest émigrés in his story two homosexual ballet dancers. Their relative happiness seems to result from their willingness to live where they are as what they are. In deciding after all not to meet Mary at the railway station, Ganin turns away from a nostalgic dream of the past, as if he, too, is now ready to live in a real present. In a sense, Nabokov does the same thing as a writer, for in his second novel, he turns away (though not permanently) from émigré life as a subject and writes instead about German characters.

The theme of perception appears in a subtle variation in *King, Queen, Knave,* when in chapter two young Franz's glasses are broken, an occurrence that offers Nabokov the opportunity to describe things impression-istically as they appear to Franz's myopic eyes. Like Kretschmar's blindness, Franz's bad eyesight also suggests danger; for Franz it is the moral danger he later encoun-ters in plotting with Martha to kill Dreyer. The original title of *Laughter in the Dark* ties the symbolism of these three novels together, for a *camera obscura* is a dark chamber such as that used for taking photographs. Nabo-kov likes the image particularly because—as is evident in the case of the sighted, then blind Kretschmar—it is sym-bolic of the chamber of human consciousness, the cham-ber in which perception takes place.

As I suggested earlier, in the Introduction and in chapter one, Nabokov's devotion to subjectivity or con-sciousness may have its roots partly in his cultural back-ground, in his family influences, or in literary preferences that he developed before he himself became a full-fledged writer. Yet one thing is certain: the extreme individualism of that attitude could only have been reinforced by the disorientation he experienced during the early years of exile. The effects of that disorientation are evident in *Speak, Memory.* According to his own description of his Cambridge years, he lived within a self-created, "arti-ficial" Russian environment, apparently making only the most casual contacts with other people. Even with his brother, Sergey, who was also at Cambridge at the time, he seems to have had a strangely distanced relationship.

Further, in a summary description of the whole exile

period before he found his "new and beloved world" in
America, Nabokov remarks that "in the course of almost
one-fifth of a century spent in Western Europe I have not
had, among the sprinkling of Germans and Frenchmen I
knew (mostly landladies and literary people), more than
two good friends." While he makes this remark after
having just stressed the compactness and cohesion of the
Russian communities of Berlin and Paris, he does not give
the impression that he had many good friends even among
his fellow émigrés.

We are not, I think, to interpret these remarks in a
sentimentally literal fashion and suppose that Nabokov
lived a sad and friendless life in those days, for he has
made it plain that *Speak, Memory* is as much a work of
art as his novels. "The following of . . . thematic designs
through one's life should be," he says, "the true purpose
of autobiography." Rather, we are to see that Nabokov's
struggle in his early years of exile to accommodate to
émigré life had a special poignancy: what future could he
have as a writer for a community of exiles who were
waiting in vain for the return of the good old days? In
the development of his Russian fiction, we can also see
evidence of Nabokov's efforts to transcend the limitations
of a career as a Russian émigré writer. The central issue
of his Russian novels is not that question about which
Alfyorov and Podtyagin argue, the "sense of this émigré
life of ours," but the greater question of the sense of life
in general.

Though the three novels just discussed all deal with
love problems, the last one marks an artistic advance for
Nabokov. In it he frames the problem of love manifestly
in terms of the theme of perception. Henceforth, his
principal themes become those of distortions in perception (as in the case of the madman or the neurotic),
unusual heightenings of perception (as in the case of the

artist), and perspectivism (variations in perception or point of view among a group of characters). At the most general level—as we shall see later on, especially in Nabokov's English fiction—these apparently separate themes become confusingly intertwined. It is as if Nabokov were asserting that the perceptual distortions of the madman and the perceptual heightenings of the artist are merely acuter versions of the difference in perspective among ordinary people.

Nabokov's short novel, *The Eye*, provides a link between the novels centered on the love problem and the later émigré fiction centered mainly on the theme of art and artistic perception, for in it Nabokov draws the two themes, love and art—or more generally, perception as affected by them—together. Various characters in *The Eye* imply that the protagonist, Smurov, is homosexual, in spite of his affairs with women. While Nabokov regards sexual aberrations as distortions of perception, he also began very early to regard such passions in an ambiguous way, sometimes suggesting that they represent the power of the human *camera obscura* to focus its sensual images to a higher than usual degree of sharpness. It is this power that the artist or the sensitive man possesses and must cultivate, whether he wants to or not.

In the case of Smurov, the love theme is clearly subordinated to the question of perception and perspective. *The Eye*, based on an all too frequent event of émigré life, the attempted suicide, reveals how far Nabokov's technical inventiveness had developed by 1930; for Smurov, who attempts suicide and lives on afterward seeing the world from the perspective of death, is not just the protagonist of the novel, but its narrator also, the "I" of *The Eye*. What Nabokov accomplishes in this work is a brilliant play on perspective. After shooting himself, Smurov continues to narrate his story, but from an oddly aesthetic perspective. No longer alive in the sense he was before, he views himself as if mirrored in the consciousnesses of the other characters. He becomes little more than his eye, an operative but not living eye that views life as a set of compositional problems or relationships.

The protagonist of *The Defense*, Luzhin, also comes to look at life as a set of compositional problems; and Nabokov concretizes Luzhin's view of life—much as he did that of the characters in *Laughter in the Dark*—by giving Luzhin a ruling passion and his story a governing metaphor. Margot manipulates Kretschmar in order to achieve success as a movie actress; film is the controlling metaphor of their lives. Luzhin's passion is chess. Alienated even as a child, Luzhin (whose name, Nabokov tells us in the introduction to the English translation, rhymes with "illusion") first gained a sense of direction and meaning in life with this obsession. Because he hides his interest, first from his parents and later from his wife, Luzhin's pleasure in the game has the tinge of erotic guilt.

For Nabokov, it seems, any interest in activity that raises human consciousness above the level of the banal or everyday reality is both a deeply pleasurable gift and a guilty burden. As a child Luzhin's sensitivity had separated him from his parents and friends. Similarly when he was becoming a chess prodigy, his detachment from his family and from life at large was increased when he fell under the management of his coach, Valentinov:

During the whole time that he [Valentinov] lived with Luzhin he unremittingly encouraged and developed his gift, not bothering for a second about Luzhin as a person, whom, it seemed, not only Valentinov but life itself had overlooked.

Luzhin's emotional starvation, a product of his obsession, leads to a mental collapse that conveniently coincides with his meeting a girl who quickly becomes his fiancée and then his wife. On the advice of a psychiatrist, Luzhin gives up chess, and his wife acts watchdog to see that he abstains from it. Luzhin is driven by the quandary of not knowing what is really real, the pure order of chess, or the corrupt chaos of life around him. He once asks his fiancée, "Are you real"; but her affirmative answer and all her pathetic efforts do not convince him in any final way. By reading chess columns in the newspaper and playing games in his head, Luzhin continues secretly to feed his old passion. Without being able to engage in actual chess matches, he is driven to see the world itself as a great chessboard on which he is playing against a mysterious and unseen opponent. Luzhin's suicide at the end is ambiguous, since it is difficult to tell whether he is a man who has saved his integrity or merely a mad suicide. His powers of concentration made him a genius, but they also consumed him.

Despair deals also with self-consuming genius; but for its protagonist, murder is the game, the fine art. In *Laughter in the Dark* the shift in narrative style at just the point where Albinus goes blind is the means by which Nabokov reinforces the contrast in the two stages of Kretschmar's affair with Margot. A similar perceptual and stylistic split occurs in *The Eye*, for there are two Smurovs, the man he is before and the ghost he is after his attempted suicide. Luzhin's life is also marked by a fatal duality, for he does not know whether the ordinary world or the chess world is real, and he suffers from the attempt to move from one to the other.

In *Despair* Nabokov takes the notion of a fatal duality in the protagonists' perception a step further and creates a dual hero. The protagonist-narrator of *Despair* is closely akin to Humbert Humbert of *Lolita*. Like Humbert, he is writing the novel to give his account of the dramatic turn his life has recently taken and to record the dissolution of a dream he had madly pursued. Like Humbert Humbert's story, Hermann's story involves the murder of a man who is very much like himself. What makes Hermann's plot significantly different from that of Humbert Humbert is that it is motivated by commonplace greed.

Hermann, the owner of a chocolate business, enjoys all the comforts of bourgeois life in Berlin. He has a pleasant little flat, a zippy blue car, and a loving but empty-headed wife named Lydia; but his business is failing. On a stroll in the country one day, he meets a laborer named Felix, who bears an astonishing physical likeness to Hermann. Hermann sees an opportunity to make a sudden windfall so that he and Lydia can retire in luxury. He kills the fatally pliant Felix after dressing him in his own clothes to make it appear that it is Hermann who has been murdered. After coaching Lydia to pretend to the police that it is really her husband who is dead, Hermann hides in a small French town near the Spanish border, using Felix's identity. There he intends to wait until the inquiry is closed, Felix is buried, and Lydia joins him with the insurance money. His plan goes wildly awry, for the supposed resemblance Felix bore to him was the product of Hermann's sick imagination.

A victim of his own distorted perception, Hermann sits in his hotel room in the little town of Pignan writing his story in an effort to discover how he slipped up. Degenerating finally into utter madness, he leaves the hotel as a crowd gathers outside. The police have arrived to take him away, and Hermann fantasizes that the whole company of people collected there are making a movie, of which he is the director. But, alas, as the date on the last few pages of his manuscript shows, he is making his movie on April Fool's Day.

Of Nabokov's three remaining Russian novels, one, *Glory*, relates to the theme of art in a strangely negative way, while another, *The Gift*, is the fullest and most straightforward treatment of the theme Nabokov had up to then produced. In *Glory*, Nabokov successfully plays an artistic game that was later to get him into trouble in his first English novel, *The Real Life of Sebastian Knight*. As if testing himself, Nabokov deliberately withholds talent from the protagonist, Martin Edelweiss. In his foreword to the English translation, Nabokov wrote:

. . . among the many gifts I showered on Martin, I was careful not to include talent. How easy it would have been to make him an artist, a writer; how hard not to let him be one, while bestowing on him the keen sensitivity that one generally associates with the creative creature. . . .

By successfully doing this, Nabokov claims to have performed his "own little exploit" within the novel. Nevertheless, the novelist's exploit was costly, for as Andrew Field has remarked (using one possible translation of the Russian novel's title), *"The Exploit* is in some respects the least exciting" of Nabokov's novels.[11] As he was later to do occasionally in his career as a writer of English fiction, Nabokov seeks relief here from the complexities of character and fictional design that are the hallmarks of most of his fiction. He not only tells Martin's story in what is for him a remarkably direct manner, but uses in it a striking amount of autobiographical material.

Like Luzhin in *The Defense*, Martin Edelweiss is an isolated man; but unlike Luzhin, he does not have an outlet for his hunger. Unfulfilled by a love affair with an older woman who only toys with him, Martin seeks out other ways to test his sense of identity. He almost dies on a mountain-climbing expedition in Switzerland. As his ultimate test, he decides to undertake a "gallant feat" (that is what the original title, *Podvig*, means), an adventurous foray into the Soviet Union. There is logic in the plan since he is a Russian émigré interested in his homeland, yet Martin's longing for Russia has less to do with the longing that other Nabokov émigrés feel than with his need for personal fulfillment.

Martin Edelweiss is, as Nabokov remarks in his introduction, his "distant cousin," with whom he shares "certain childhood memories, certain later likes and dislikes." Critics have pointed out the extensive parallels between passages in the novel describing Martin's life and passages in *Speak, Memory* describing Nabokov's own life.[12] There is, however, a much closer affinity between Nabokov and Fyodor Godunov-Cherdyntsev, the brilliant writer in *The Gift*. All the talent that Nabokov denied Martin, he lavished on Fyodor, so that they are, the author and his character, more like fraternal twins.

As *The Gift* opens, Godunov-Cherdyntsev, a Russian émigré in Berlin, has just published a book of poems, and the early pages of *The Gift* deal with the beginnings of his career as a poet. Very soon, however, Godunov-Cherdyntsev's desire to recapture the memory of his father becomes an intrusive concern; and like the narrator of Nabokov's first English novel, *The Real Life of Sebastian Knight*, he becomes engrossed in the problems of balance and accuracy that are involved in the writing of biography. In its own way *The Gift* also centers on the problems of perspective that are present in Nabokov's other Russian fiction; but here they are more explicitly related to the writer's craft. The biography of his father is never actually written, but Godunov-Cherdyntsev does gather material for it and weighs and compares the different images of his father he gets from diverse sources (an encyclopedia is one source, his mother is another). Further, he does write a biography of a nineteenth-cen-

tury critic and revolutionary named Chernyshevski, which
is actually included in *The Gift* as the long chapter four
(of five chapters). Because he is a poet, Godunov-Cherdyntsev writes poetic history.

In his story Nabokov illustrates a principle that he
enunciated many years later, in 1970, when he remarked
that history does not exist apart from the historian.[13]
Since the subjectivizing of biography or history is inevitable anyway, the best biography will be brightened by an
author with a brilliant mind and style. Having failed to
write his father's biography, Godunov-Cherdyntsev succeeds with Chernyshevski; and having succeeded and
resolved the problem that biography represented, he can
continue his career as an artist more freely.

A "bookish" novel in many ways, *The Gift* represents Nabokov's summing up of his own literary struggles
during the émigré period. Like *Ada*, which may be considered its counterpart for Nabokov's career as an English-language novelist, *The Gift* is densely allusive and for
that reason less accessible to the general reader. Both
novels are summations, thirty or so years apart, of Nabokov's conception of the writer's profession. They are, in a
sense, books for fellow writers and for Nabokov lovers.

Though not last in the order of composition of the
Russian novels, *Invitation to a Beheading* is nevertheless
an appropriate novel for launching the discussions of
Nabokov's English fiction; for in it Nabokov depicts in
the starkest possible terms the basic tension of all his
fiction—the elemental tension between life and death, creation and dissolution. Even the embracing themes of life
and art are subsumed by this one, for they are simply
ways of expressing the life principle and of thwarting
death. From the start, Cincinnatus (the protagonist of
Invitation) knows that he must die, why he must die, and
how; what he does not know is when. Like the Russian

émigrés in the other novels, he is waiting; but because he knows exactly what it is he is waiting for, his life is a period of unrelieved tension. His concentration on that one coming moment and the fact of approaching death leaves little room for the sense of ordinary reality to develop.

Shunned in school and later by his fellow workers in the doll factory, he finds a human response only in Marthe. After they are married Marthe openly indulges in affairs. Because Cincinnatus is generally recognized as a peculiar person, no one blames Marthe. What Cincinnatus has that others fear and hate so much is a mind. His mind is a *camera obscura* in which the external world is so sharply focused as to reveal its incredible unreality. He is shunned because he has an interior life and a power of penetration that no one else understands. Cincinnatus's crime is the opacity of his soul, the very nature of his being. Yet in Nabokov's view Cincinnatus's opacity is the sign of life; and though he is headed for death and darkness at the end, the soulless and unmysterious beings around him are as good as dead already.

At the novel's startling conclusion, Nabokov grants Cincinnatus his freedom. As the executioner begins the downswing of his ax, Cincinnatus, refusing to submit, rises from the block and walks away. His refusal to cooperate with the mad world's illusion of the necessity of his own death represents the triumph of his opaque soul over those around him. The triumph of the powers of consciousness forms a basic assumption in all that Nabokov subsequently writes, the English novels included. In addition, Cincinnatus's wait for death finds its way—in many guises and variations—into all the English novels Nabokov goes on to write.

3

Fables of Genius:
The Real Life
of Sebastian Knight
and Bend Sinister

Nabokov's fiction is peopled by characters whose spiritual hungers make them highly vulnerable to illusions. This one quality unites his various protagonists, and the probing of their illusions constitutes his greatest theme. This preoccupation has important consequences for Nabokov's art. First, by means of such probing, he forces his fiction beyond the in some ways simpler modes of tragedy and comedy toward the more complex mode of irony. To be sure, the probing of illusions is also an integral part of both comedy and tragedy; but those modes move typically toward quite recognizable and solid resolutions. In each case illusion is exorcised by reality, the exorcism leading in one to a happy ending and in the other to a sad one.

There is a wealth of comic and tragic touches in Nabokov's fiction; but the controlling mode is irony, and irony has its own special requirements. For the ironist there is no ultimate and solid reality that is not itself subject to attack as an illusion. Hence, any work controlled by irony is necessarily robbed of that sense of finality that makes up a large share of the pleasure of comedy and tragedy. Nabokov's commitment to irony not only produces his famous inconclusive conclusions, but also constantly reminds us of the uncertainty of fate.

The desire to probe illusions has a notable effect on characterization, especially for Nabokov. To a writer of his sophisticated tastes, the testing of illusions can be genuinely interesting only if the major characters are strong. Nabokov usually measures the strength of his characters either by their ability to resist the illusions of others (even poor Lolita is strong in this sense) or by their ability to create illusions of their own (most of Nabokov's madmen have this power). Nabokov's favorite characters possess both kinds of strength. Though this does not make them proof against the antics of fate, it makes their struggle slightly more even and far more interesting. Nabokov's concern with this sort of strength leads him quite naturally to write about artists, geniuses, and the especially gifted, and seldom, if ever, about ordinary man, whose existence—in Nabokov's view—is merely hypothetical anyway.

In general, Nabokov's first two English-language novels, *The Real Life of Sebastian Knight* and *Bend Sinister*, do not seem to have much in common. The former purports to be a critical biography; the latter, a story of totalitarian oppression. Though one was written in Paris and the other in Cambridge, Massachusetts, both novels grew out of Nabokov's experiences during the years of his European exile, from 1919 to 1940. Many autobiographical ties are readily recognizable. Nabokov has revealed in *Speak, Memory* that the story of V and his brother Sebastian is an evocation of Nabokov's own curiosity about his brother Sergey. In the memoir, Nabokov wrote with a quiet sadness about Sergey, who unfortunately remained in Europe and died in "a Hamburg concentration camp . . . on January 10, 1945."

Sergey's life may have been the partial basis for *Sebastian Knight*, just as his death partially accounts for the mood of *Bend Sinister*. It was only a matter of months after Sergey's death that Nabokov began work (in the winter of 1945) on his second English novel, which presents a savage vision of the kind of insane regime that killed Sergey Nabokov. *Bend Sinister* represents the life Nabokov knew in Germany under the shadow of approaching Nazism and illustrates his awareness of the conditions of life imposed both in Russia by the communists and in Germany by Hitler.

Beyond the autobiographical connections, one can observe a subtle but significant interplay of theme and method in the two novels. While *Sebastian Knight* seems highly individual in theme and *Bend Sinister* highly political, the novels are in actuality odd inversions of each other and for that reason make interesting companion pieces. *Sebastian Knight*, presumably a biography written from a personal inner knowledge of the subject, collapses into a strange and unsatisfying impersonality. *Bend Sinister*, whose theme is presumably social and political in scope, creates a personal portrait far more concrete and compelling. Each in its own way—and with a different degree of success—is an examination of the lives of geniuses and of the illusions to which they are subject.

The plot of *Sebastian Knight* centers around a moderately known fiction writer, whose life story is narrated by his half-brother, identified only by the initial "V." The brothers, both, like Nabokov, born in Russia around the turn of the century, had the same father; but Sebastian's mother was an English woman who had abandoned the son and husband, while V's mother was the father's second wife, a Russian woman with whom he apparently had a happy marriage. In 1913 the father died in a peculiarly motivated duel to defend his first wife's honor, and six years later the rest of the family fled the Bolsheviks, V and his mother taking up residence in Paris, while Sebastian enrolled in Cambridge University.

V was compelled to write the book, which he commenced two months after Sebastian's death in 1936, by several motives. Partly he wrote to express for the dead brother an honestly felt affection that he had been unable to express before. Because Sebastian had always remained "silent and distant," V had never known or understood him very well. In fact, V learned far more about Sebastian from reading his novels than he had ever learned from personal contact. The fascination with this paradox—of having gotten more of Sebastian from art than from reality—resulted in another strong motive for writing the book—to defend his brother against the images of him produced by others. In particular, he wrote in reaction to a book, *The Tragedy of Sebastian Knight*, by Sebastian's former secretary and literary agent, Mr. Goodman.

V strives in the real story of Sebastian to protect his brother's memory from a variety of actual and potential distortions. Goodman's book had two principal faults, one moral, the other intellectual. First it is clear that V regards Goodman as an opportunist, a crass commercial hack anxious to profit from the brief association he had had with Sebastian and to publish his book before the grass has had time to grow over Sebastian's grave. The intellectual fault is Goodman's commitment to fashionable and shallow ideas. His book is a historicist work, that is, one founded on a philosophy of history that holds that each age has its individual character and that every product of a given age bears the stamp of that character. V rejects as "rubbish" Goodman's "thick flow of philosophical treacle" and his contention that Sebastian was a "victim of his time." Quite apart from his dislike of Goodman, V scorns the idea of historicism because it focuses on common qualities and refuses to recognize the unique.

In a visit with his and Sebastian's old Swiss governess to gather material for the book, V confronted another kind of distortion, though this one involved no real culpability. Senile Mademoiselle, then in her seventies, was no help because her memory was failing and she could not keep even the simplest details straight. At the close of their interview, she urged V to write a "beautiful book" about Sebastian: ". . . make it a fairy-tale with Sebastian for prince. The enchanted prince. . . ."

V's *Real Life of Sebastian Knight* is meant as a corrective of the sorts of distortions represented by Good-

man and Mademoiselle, and the fundamental principal
behind his enterprise is a recognition of the essentially
paradoxical nature of Sebastian's genius. "Sebastian's
constant aloofness," a quality often noted by others, made
him socially awkward. In one of his books, Sebastian
described himself appropriately as a "colour-blind cha-
meleon." That is, wanting to be loved like everyone else,
he was willing to adapt, but at the same time innately
unable to do so. V elaborates the idea:

The keynote of Sebastian's life was solitude and the
kindlier fate tried to make him feel at home by counterfeiting
admirably the things he thought he wanted, the more he was
aware of his inability to fit into the picture,—into any kind
of picture.

Sebastian's efforts at social adaptation seem to have
been balked by the richness and power of his interior life.
He lived inwardly at a rate far faster than that of most
people. V quotes Sebastian on the point:

Most brains have their Sundays, mine was even refused a
half-holiday. This state of constant wakefulness was extremely painful not only in itself, but in its direct results.
Every ordinary act which, as a matter of course, I had to
perform, took on such a complicated appearance, provoked
such a multitude of associative ideas in my mind, and these
associations were so tricky and obscure, so utterly useless
for practical application, that I would either shirk the
business at hand or else make a mess out of it out of sheer
nervousness.

Sebastian's awkwardness was not the ordinary adolescent kind. It was a permanent state, experienced for most
of his early years as a liability, before—by the kind of
miracle Nabokov likes to write about—Sebastian managed to convert it into an advantage. It was at Cambridge
that Sebastian gave up trying to "fit into the picture,"

yielded finally to the powers of his own mind, and turned them to artistic profit. There he "grimly started to cultivate self-consciousness as if it had been some rare talent or passion," and gained "satisfaction from its rich and monstrous growth, ceasing to worry about his awkward uncongeniality." So much evidence of Sebastian's talent is offered, largely by means of quotations from his works, that no reader is likely to deny his genius. Sebastian Knight's literary power is supposed to qualify him for the dominant place in *The Real Life of Sebastian Knight*; but because the drama of the novel belongs more properly to V rather than to Sebastian, the latter's talent proves more troublesome than helpful.

The novel is built on a central combination of perceptions: that the hyperactive mind is both the artist's burden and his gift and, further, that the success of art depends on its creator's ability to yield to his own genius. Oddly enough, these very principles balk the novel's progress and make of *Sebastian Knight* a flawed masterpiece, an interesting failure.

Nabokov himself has spoken of the book's "unbearable imperfections."[1] While this is much too strong, his colorfully metaphoric reference, in *Speak, Memory*, to its "gloriettes and self-mate combinations" offers a valuable critical clue to the novel's problems. The terms are drawn from architecture and from chess. A gloriette is a highly ornamented chamber, and by "gloriettes" Nabokov refers to the novel's fancy writing. Like all his works, *Sebastian Knight* is full of brilliant descriptions, but quite unlike his other works, the overall design of this one is self-defeating. The novel "check-mates" itself. In analyzing his brother's art, V says that in Sebastian's fiction it is "not the parts" that matter, but "their combinations." The same principle, when applied to *Sebastian Knight*, reveals the novel's basic flaw.

What slows the story's movement—especially in the first half—is the peculiar lack of tension or motive force that results from V's suppression of his own powers. Though Nabokov has allowed V to perceive the yielding-to-genius principle behind Sebastian's success, he has not allowed V to exercise his own genius. This might not prove destructive except for two important facts. First, the tactic appears illogical in light of the novel's conclusion. There Nabokov played his game of character-doubling. In a surprise ending that is the novel's strongest feature, V claims more than the "inner knowledge" of Sebastian he has said he possessed all along. He claims identity with Sebastian. Second, the tactic does not appear to take into account the fact that Nabokov's talent is essentially that of a stylist. Any plan that limits his use of that talent in a work is bound to hamper the story's development. All his characters must be "little Nabokovs" to one degree or another; and certainly all his narrators must be themselves superb stylists.

The object of V's self-suppression (or Nabokov's suppression of him) is intelligible enough. Such a limitation is intended to induce by contrast a vivid image of Sebastian. By assaulting the reader with dazzling quotations from Sebastian's works, V allows the brilliance of Sebastian's writing to shine forth against the simplicity of his own. Such a procedure is much too negative. The more V tries to evoke an impression of his brother's genius, the more the potential of the basic materials dwindles. What looked at first like a stroke of genius, Nabokov's submersion of himself into the persona of an inexperienced and merely adequate writer, threatens to destroy the novel. Stylist that he is, Nabokov cannot long write plainly.

In the first half of *Sebastian Knight*, the occasional instances of poor articulation on V's part (the blatant use of a weak intensive in chapter two, the string of obviously planted clichés in chapter four) suggest the deliberateness of the suppression. Yet V manages to sneak in two "gloriettes" of his own: a striking one-paragraph vignette at the opening of chapter 3, which describes the family's tense escape from Russia, and a vivid set piece late in chapter fourteen, which languidly evokes Sebastian's first adolescent love affair. It is only when Nabokov abandons the suppressive strategy that he partly rescues the novel from its doldrums.

The novel changes gears at midpoint, and the plot moves through two dramatic phases. While in the first half, V's role was limited essentially to collecting and recording evidence of Sebastian's genius, Nabokov at last involved him actively in a drama of his own. Suddenly the critical biography is transmuted into a mystery story, complete with a detective (retired, but still helpful) and a culprit (identified by the mystery story's typical process of elimination and a clever verbal ruse on V's part).

Performing a customary duty of the next of kin, V burns (according to Sebastian's wishes) two packets of love letters Sebastian had received. One was from Clare Bishop, whose affair with Sebastian had lasted six years and whose loyal affection had been a positive force in Sebastian's life. The other packet was from a mysterious Russian woman for whom he had inexplicably abandoned Clare. Sebastian's second affair had been brief and negative. It symbolized to V the fatality that colored Sebastian's "last and saddest years." The novel's second phase (chapters eleven through seventeen) is devoted to tracking down the mysterious mistress, not for purposes of revenge, but so that V can better understand his brother. Though he manages to find her (a seductive adventuress, she is now married to an older man with whom she is obviously bored) and thus solves the factual puzzle of her identity, he cannot express directly the reasons for Sebastian's attraction to her. V's description of the relationship of Sebastian and Nina Toorovetz is cast in terms of the relation of art to life.

The contrast between Sebastian's two mature love affairs has thematic point. Sebastian's way of life was peculiar, from the ordinary perspective. Burdened by his creativity, he learned the value of subordinating his external "realistic" life to his internal "artistic" life. Once he had voluntarily endorsed this state of affairs (which because of the power of his genius was a necessity), his existence was smoother. Into this pattern Clare Bishop had readily fit, entering his life without drama or fun, making no demands, and offering him loving support. But the comfortable affair with Clare was abruptly replaced by the turbulent one with Nina, who found Sebastian amusing at first, then tedious, and finally refused to see him. Whereas Clare had happily accepted Sebastian's commitment to art and the consequent subordination of life in his scale of priorities, Nina preferred adventures in the external world and quickly grew bored with Sebastian.

After meeting her, V has a metaphor for Nina (she is a bat, blind to the beauty of art and to the genius of the man she had discarded), but he has no *real* explanation for Sebastian's behavior. He ends up offering the reader a conundrum: "Two modes of his [Sebastian's] life question each other and the answer is his life itself, and that is the nearest one can ever approach a human truth." Reduced to its simplest terms, this vatic utterance means that the "real life" of Sebastian Knight is founded on a principle of irony. In his early years, when he still tried to find his place in life, he doubted the reality of his inner world and fought its domination. External reality questioned internal reality then. Later, however, when he yielded to his own genius, the inner reality was dominant and questioned the external one. In his later years, drawn mysteriously by Nina Toorovetz out of the comforts of one fairly settled mode of life back toward the other, Sebastian Knight began to recognize the irony of his own existence. In his last works, he wrote more and more frequently of the fatality (a product of that irony) that haunts even the happiest and freest experiences of life.

The preceding description of the narrative's movement suggests, at least by implication, one of the novel's most striking oddities, the continual shifts of tense and time frame. The narrative moves back and forth between past-tense descriptions of events in Sebastian's life and past- and present-tense descriptions of the events that led up to V's decision to write the story and of the steps by which V pursued his task. Instead of the straight-forward past-tense narration one expects in biography, one gets a peculiar mixture of fiction and exposition, of anecdotes about Sebastian and quotations from his works, as well as V's reflections on his brother's life and on his own experiences while working on the book. While the novel occasionally exhibits the Nabokovian stylistic sparkle, it is damaged by the disjointedness of its narrative procedure. Satisfying to the reader in parts, it is frustrating as a whole.

In its final phase the novel moves to a peak of tension that is all the stronger for the flaccidity of the first half. The last two chapters record, in the present tense, V's frenzied efforts to reach the dying Sebastian, who he believes will impart to him "a striking disclosure" or "some extraordinary revelation." The success of this moving conclusion is due to the final blossoming of V's own narrative and descriptive power. Fully released from the earlier suppression, V describes in Kafkaesque dreamlike fashion his confusion at receiving the news of Sebastian's failing condition, the indecision about suddenly abandoning his job and setting out to see Sebastian, the self-created frustration of having left behind the address of the doctor, the oppressive crush of human bodies on the train that reminds him of the frailties of the flesh.

Arriving much later than he had hoped at the hospital in a remote French village, V himself becomes the novel's final victim of irony. Inwardly expressing his joy at having arrived in time, V discovers that the man near whose bed he sits is not his brother after all. The nurse was confused. Sebastian had died the day before.

In the search for a satisfactory understanding of *The Real Life of Sebastian Knight*, one is tempted to try to resolve the difficulties by arguing that the true protagonist is V rather than Sebastian. Such a reading could be buttressed by the novel's final lines: "I am Sebastian, or Sebastian is I, or perhaps we are both someone whom neither of us knows." The novel's point would then be that what Sebastian had discovered at Cambridge—that his awkwardness and estrangement had a positive meaning, that is, that he is an artist—is what V discovers about himself in the act of writing his book. Yet this reading leads to other difficulties, for V's assertion of himself and his own storytelling power toward the novel's close is less convincing when viewed as a result of V's self-realization than when viewed as Nabokov's need to infuse drama into a sluggish story. Besides, the final lines stretch far beyond a simple identification of Sebastian and V to dissolve their suddenly discovered common identity into the ungraspable mystery of being in general. This dissolution robs a perilously hollow novel of its concreteness, just when that concreteness is beginning to gel. This frustration of its own potential is the novel's ultimate "self-mate combination."

In spite of its failings, however, *The Real Life of Sebastian Knight* has been highly praised by such distinguished admirers as Herbert Gold, Erskine Caldwell, Howard Nemerov, and Flannery O'Connor.

In *Bend Sinister* Nabokov took up once again the themes he had unfolded in *Sebastian Knight*: the burden of genius, the play of illusions. But in the later novel, there are saving differences. The narrative strategy Nabokov chose for *Sebastian Knight* proved an awkward limitation on the exercise of not only his talent as stylist but also that as ironist. For the greater part of *Sebastian Knight*, no posited reality (neither that of Sebastian nor that of V) is sufficiently solid (that is, sufficiently backed by Nabokov's potent prose) for its illusiveness to be exposed with suitable force. Instead of the leisurely gathering of images that marks the first half of *Sebastian Knight*, Nabokov immediately presents the reader of *Bend Sinister* with a veil of vivid images, whose density makes the game of illusions a convincing challenge from the outset. The novel begins with a bravura passage that evokes a sense of depth and tension that the earlier work achieved only at its climax. (*Bend Sinister* opens with a scene in a hospital, just as *Sebastian Knight* closes with one.)

The first chapter consists of ten short paragraphs thick with descriptive details intended to reflect the main character's momentary perceptions, in the middle of which rests a single sentence that sets the plot in motion. Amidst such vivid images as those of "[a]n oblong puddle inset in the coarse asphalt," the "pale blue sky," the "dappled surfaces" of a house across from the hospital, "the dull green of the narrow lawn," and the trees "with their trillions of twigs"—amidst the richness of this color and life that engage the protagonist's senses lies the sim-

ple observation that moves his heart and mind: "The
operation has not been successful and my wife will die."

These perceptions and this prediction belong to
Adam Krug, a brilliant middle-aged philosopher, citizen
of a European country that has just undergone a totalitarian revolution whose leaders are settling apprehensive-
ly into power. The opening chapter's striking juxtaposition of Krug's perceptions with his recognition of the
harsh fact of his wife's impending death indicates that he
—like Sebastian Knight—is besieged by the importun-
ities of the inner and outer worlds. The pressure of these
competing demands and their companion responsibilities
grows ever more intense as the novel develops, until
Nabokov—who appears at last in his own narratorial person—mercifully allows Adam Krug to go mad, thus
relieving him of his burden.

Nabokov must have learned a good deal from the
experience of writing *Sebastian Knight*, for the deficien-
cies of that work are matched by the strengths of *Bend
Sinister*. First, there is one principal character, the genius
Krug. Second, Nabokov has told Krug's story in the third
person, adopting intermittently a modified stream-of-con-
sciousness technique so that his brilliant descriptive passages may represent the creative acts of Krug's own mind.
Third, this wise consolidation of effects makes the world
of Adam Krug real enough for that world's final ironic
demolition to be extremely moving.

The portrait of the protagonist contributes a good
deal to the novel's success. Nabokov has made Adam
Krug much tougher and stronger than Sebastian Knight,
and also placed him in a circumstantially more lifelike
context. Sebastian was an artist who lived not on the
fruits of his labor, but on an inheritance from his mother.
He was thus able to maintain an easier independence of
the world and could lightly sweep aside all promptings to

take part in the world's affairs. No less a genius. than Sebastian, Adam Krug gets involved in politics, even though he lives in an academic ivory tower. As the most respected member of the faculty at the University of Padukgrad, his country's recently renamed capital city, Krug is pressed by his colleagues to lead the university's conciliation with the new regime. Without such conciliation, the university—like other prerevolutionary institutions—has no future, nor does its faculty. Aside from Krug's professional prestige (he is the only scholar on the faculty with a worldwide reputation), he is qualified in the eyes of the university's president for his ambassadorial mission by the fact that he was once a classmate of the revolutionary chief, Paduk.

Not only has Nabokov given Krug's life a responsible professional context, but a responsible domestic context as well. At the same time that his colleagues are pressing him to carry their propitiatory declaration to Paduk, Krug must arrange for the burial of his beloved wife, Olga, and deal with the problem of how to tell their eight-year-old David about her death. By locating his protagonist at the center of personal, professional, and national crises, Nabokov immediately conjured up a dramatic tension, whose force far surpasses anything the protagonist of *Sebastian Knight* (whether Sebastian or V) must confront.

To heighten the drama, Nabokov has made Krug seem more than equal to the challenge, by giving the reader a full, if compressed, picture of his physical and mental makeup. Whereas Sebastian Knight allowed himself to be intimidated (certainly in his youth, but even later in the love affair with Nina Toorovetz) by his own special awkwardness, Adam Krug always speaks his mind, and the intelligence of his opinions wins the admiration of others, though those opinions are occasionally offensive. While Sebastian Knight seems to exist in the rather thin atmosphere of a *fin-de-siècle* aestheticism and his love life seems like the airy intercourse of Milton's disembodied angels, Adam Krug is a powerful and virile man, as capable of crudeness and vulgarity as of the highest flights of the mind. He has, Nabokov says, "a queer streak of vulgarity and even cruelty." Late in the novel Krug's young housekeeper tries to seduce him. His response to her teasing suggests, for one thing, the degree of verisimilitude of his portrait:

You know too little or much too much. If too little, then run along, lock yourself up, never come near me because this is going to be a bestial explosion, and you might get badly hurt. I warn you. I am nearly three times your age and a great big sad hog of a man. And I don't love you.

Not only does this passage suggest Adam Krug's root-edness in the physical, but it also implies a sexual violence that parallels a similar violence in the operations of his mind. Krug's warning to the girl that she can expect no sexual restraint from him is analogous to the insistence on intellectual freedom that gets him into political trouble.

In the half-dozen or so years between the writing of *Sebastian Knight* and the writing of *Bend Sinister*, Nabokov's fictional technique seems to have acquired a notable sharpness and clarity. In *Bend Sinister* there is no fading away into conundrums. The contrast between Sebastian Knight and Adam Krug is, if anything, even fuller on the mental level than on the physical. Though all of V's quotations from Sebastian's works are presumably intro-duced to demonstrate Sebastian's genius, the tendency toward pretentious proverbs that they reveal is less a sign of Sebastian's wisdom than a mark of his intellectual weakness. V does the memory of his brother no real service by stringing together such quotations as this:

All things belong to the same order of things, for such is
the oneness of human perception, the oneness of individuality,
the oneness of matter, whatever matter may be. The only
real number is one, the rest are mere repetition.

A quarter of a century later, in an interview with
Alfred Appel in 1966, Nabokov indirectly scorned Sebastian's shallow and puerile profundities. "Aphoristicism,"
he said, "is a sign of arteriosclerosis."[2] (One should not,
of course, overlook the fact that Nabokov's assertion is
itself a proverb mocking proverbs.) Long before that,
however, he had expressed the criticism artistically by
counterbalancing Sebastian's mental thinness with Adam
Krug's intellectual solidity.

Chapter fourteen of *Bend Sinister* offers in the
thoughts of Krug a direct rebuff to Sebastian's philosophical naiveté:

He had never indulged in the search for True Substance,
the One, the Absolute, the Diamond suspended from the
Christmas Tree of the Cosmos. He had always felt the faint
ridicule of a finite mind peering at the iridescence of the
invisible through the prison bars of integers. And even if the
thing could be sought, why should he, or anybody else for
that matter, wish the phenomenon to lose its curls, its mask,
its mirror, and become the bald noumenon?

Although Sebastian's aphorisms contain ideas similar to
those of Adam Krug, their value is heavily compromised
by the immaturity of Sebastian's expression of them, compromised in fact by the very effort to express them.

Steadily throughout *Bend Sinister*, Nabokov has
developed the impression of Krug's intellectual power.
His close friend and colleague, Ember, admiringly char-
acterizes Krug's mind early in the story: "Krug could
take aim at a flock of the most popular and sublime human
thoughts and bring down a wild goose any time." Krug

himself explains his intellectual values later to a young colleague, who awkwardly suggests that Krug probably places himself higher than his colleagues in his own esteem: "I esteem my colleagues as I do my own self, I esteem them for two things: because they are able to find perfect felicity in specialized knowledge and because they are not apt to commit physical murder."

These standards are what make Krug's compromise with the new government impossible. The regime was founded on a parody of communism known as "Ekwilism" (equalism), whose triumphant theory was successfully propagated by Paduk's revolutionary Party of the Average Man. As laid down by its originator and Paduk's patron, Fradrick Skotoma, the doctrine of Ekwilism held that at any given time there is "a certain computable amount of human consciousness distributed throughout the population of the world" and that the unevenness of its distribution is "the root of all our woes." There should be, according to Ekwilism, no individual "with more brains or guts than others." Such a doctrine conflicts with the intellectual requirements necessary for finding what Krug appreciates, "perfect felicity in specialized knowledge." To his sorrow Krug also finds that the leaders of the regime do not qualify for his respect on the other ground either. In the reign of terror they institute to quell opposition, they are more than willing "to commit physical murder."

The stages of the novel's plot are marked by the arrest and imprisonment of all of Krug's friends, one after the other, as the regime seeks to find "a handle" to compel Krug's cooperation. Krug is cornered, both by his colleagues, who betray the principal of intellectual freedom and urge him to make peace with the regime for their sake, and by the revolutionaries, who court his favor, hoping his renown will help legitimize their rule in the eyes of the world. In two scenes full of the kind of comic grotesquery for which Nabokov is justly famous, Adam Krug rejects both the document he is asked to sign by his colleagues and the contract offered him by Paduk to become the well-paid president of the university.

A large part of the comic effect of those scenes rests on the degree to which Krug is—as he says himself—"a slave of images." He cannot forget, either in the meeting with his importunate colleagues or in the interview with Paduk, that he and his classmates as adolescents had thoroughly disliked Paduk, who was then their peer. Paduk's unpopularity derives from no specifiable vice, but from the general physical and mental unhealthiness his fellows sensed in him even then. Though everyone else is willing to do so, including the new leader himself, Krug cannot forget that he and his friends used to call Paduk the Toad and that Krug in particular used to enjoy the sport of sitting on the Toad's face.

All the pressures people apply to him are applied on the assumption (especially paradoxical for the Ekwilist side) that the genius can solve their problems. Krug holds out in stolid independence as long as he can. Refusing to compromise at all, he occupies a position of pained and detached bemusement, all the while constantly returning in thought to his personal grief. Puncturing at one point the university president's notion that he and Paduk were formerly great friends, he calls the idea a "sentimental delusion."

Later, when the pressure has had more time to build, Krug meditates on his predicament, wondering how he, with his total lack of interest in politics, has become the crux of a power play. He wonders how he, the detached philosopher, can be expected to solve the problems that are destroying his world. The conclusion that he reaches is that he himself is quite unreal. He begins "to regard himself as an illusion or rather a shareholder in an illusion which was highly appreciated by a great number of cultured people (with a generous sprinkling of semi-cultured ones)." Now—as a coveted, though still uncooperative pawn of the regime—he has become an illusion of the totally uncultured, the Ekwilists.

What others do not seem to see—though Krug quite clearly does—is that his kind of genius cannot be used as a positive instrument or agency. His gift is one for "creative destruction," an endless cyclical process of ground clearing and building structures of critical analysis. What he possesses is not so much a philosophy as an ability; not so much opinions and views, as an attitude.

For a time, it looks as if Krug's ungraspability (or what one might call, adopting the metaphor of the novel, his handlelessness) is also a "sentimental delusion." At the novel's terrifying conclusion, Krug is arrested and his son separated from him. Though he quickly capitulates to all the Ekwilists' demands in an effort to save David, he is thwarted by a fatal mixup in which David is killed in a revoltingly bestial psychological experiment at a state hospital (a gripping nightmare-shadow of Nazi atrocities). Paduk offers Krug all kinds of unimaginable forms of restitution, including the pleasure of murdering David's murderers. In a walled courtyard (a symbolic setting woven throughout the story to suggest Krug's desolation), Krug has a final opportunity to capitulate, this time to save the lives of twenty-four prisoners, four of whom are his closest friends. Under this final pressure, Krug cracks, and his beseeching friends realize "with a shock that they [are] addressing a madman." At the end, mad Adam Krug is shot as he suddenly reverts to his adolescent game and tries to chase down the Toad one more time. Nothing can touch him any longer.

The Real Life of Sebastian Knight is perhaps an unintentional parody of Sebastian's last novel, *The Doubtful Asphodel*, the theme of which, according to V, is a man dying. *Bend Sinister* is, by contrast, the story of a dying and finally dead world that cannot be warmed back to meaningful life even by the vital humanity of the genius-hero.

Bend Sinister is Nabokov's first significant achievement as an English-language novelist. Its world is solid and tangible, and Adam Krug is one of the strongest of Nabokov's characters, including those in his Russian fiction. Because Krug and his world are so solid, however, the reader tends to do what Nabokov wants most for him to avoid, that is, make value judgments. To solve this problem, Nabokov closed the novel with a technical trick. In the last four paragraphs, he suddenly broke the fictional illusion of his work by switching from a description of Krug's final moments to a description of himself as a writer in his room working on the novel. The illusion is broken and Nabokov reminds the reader that art is, after all, a game and judgments are inappropriate:

He [Krug] saw the Toad crouching at the foot of the wall, shaking, dissolving, speeding up his shrill incantations, protecting his dimming face with his transparent arm, and Krug ran towards him, and just a fraction of an instant before another and better bullet hit him, he shouted again: You, you—and the wall vanished, like a rapidly withdrawn slide, and I stretched myself and got up from among the chaos of written and rewritten pages, to investigate the sudden twang that something had made in striking the wire netting of my window.

4

....

Aesthetic Bliss:

Lolita

In these days when "average" housewives and business-men, as well as confirmed lechers, frequent X-rated movies and bring suit against the state to challenge laws proscribing various forms of sexual behavior, it is difficult to understand the American reading public's shocked response to the publication of *Lolita* in 1958. Yet not since the 1933 court battle over the publication of James Joyce's *Ulysses* had there been such a vigorous moral stir about a novel. Unprepared, and by present-day standards "prudish," readers were once disturbed by the explicitness of Joyce's treatment of bodily functions, adultery, masturbation, and a variety of erotic fantasies. One would have thought that the general acceptance of *Ulysses* and similar works by the 1950s would have smoothed the way for *Lolita*, but such was not the case. The titles of some of the first reviews suggest the nature of the response: "Lolita, at 12, Makes Scarlett O'Hara Turn Forever Amber" (Houston *Press*); " 'Lolita' May Give You the Creeps" (Minneapolis *Sunday Tribune*); "A Superb Writer Fashions a Work of Art on a Questionable Theme" (Sacramento *Bee*); "Sex—Without the Asterisks" (*Esquire*); "Through the Taste Barrier" (*Manchester Guardian*).[1]

Even sophisticated readers, whose assumptions about the morality of art had already been remarkably liberalized by one hundred and fifty years of the influence of romantic idealism, were uncertain about the novel's propriety. Readers who could quite readily accept Satan as the hero of *Paradise Lost* (as the Romantics taught us to do) or willingly plunge into the morbid depths of the decadent imagination (say, into Baudelaire's *Les Fleurs du mal*) were still disturbed by *Lolita*. From the perspective of the present, it is tempting to view *Lolita* as a brilliant coup, for Nabokov constructed his novel upon the violation of a taboo, just before the floodgates of permissiveness or liberality (depending on your viewpoint) were thrown open.

The plot is deceptively simple. Humbert Humbert is a refined and scholarly minded European who has long masked his illicit passion for little girls by carrying on unsatisfying love affairs with grown women. After settling into a compromise marriage with a girlish woman named Valeria, he learns that a rich uncle in the United States has left him an income on condition that he move to the States. At about the same time, he learns that the equally unsatisfied Valeria has taken a lover and prefers to remain in Europe.

Sailing alone to the United States, Humbert fatefully moves into the sleepy New England town of Ramsdale, as the boarder of the widow Charlotte Haze. Charlotte has a delectable twelve-year-old daughter and a hunger for male companionship. Handsome Humbert's opportunity is made to order. He marries the mother to remain near the daughter; and after the mother's accidental death, he spirits Lolita away. To avoid the watchful eyes of Ramsdale neighbors, the middle-aged Humbert and his teen-aged stepdaughter and mistress crisscross the United States on a trip of several thousand miles, returning East to settle for a time in Beardsley so that Lolita can go to school and at least appear to be living like other girls of her age. Humbert's luck does not last, for Lolita is stolen away from him (she cooperates with her abductor) by Clare Quilty, who is impotent, but in Humbert's eyes far more perverted than Humbert himself.

After an unsuccessful two-year search for her, Humbert receives a letter from Lolita and goes to visit her. Instead of the cherished nymphet, he finds a faded, unappealing, pregnant sixteen-year-old housewife married to one Richard Schiller. After learning that it was Quilty who had stolen her from him, Humbert seeks out his old rival and kills him for revenge. The novel, whose subtitle is "The Confessions of a White Widowed Male," is Humbert Humbert's first-person account of his love story, written in jail while he awaits trial for the murder of Quilty. Humbert dies before his trial, never imagining that his Lolita will die shortly afterward in childbirth, (a fact that the reader has learned from John Ray, the fictitious editor, in the foreword to the work). In his closing lines, Humbert offers the book as a monument to his love for Lolita.

What makes all of this something more than either a case study of sexual perversion or pornographic titillation is the truly shocking fact that Humbert Humbert is a genius who, through the power of his artistry, actually persuades the reader that his memoir is a love story. It is this accomplishment that makes the novel a surprising success from the perspective of Humbert Humbert's desires and intentions. From the perspective of Nabokov's and the reader's desires and intentions, *Lolita* fulfills the highest standards of artistic perfection in the organic fusion of its fable and its form.

The fable of *Lolita* can best be understood in the light of two theories of human behavior, one drawn from the history of ideas, the other from contemporary psychology. First, Humbert Humbert's love story makes sense against the background of the kind of "emotional archaeology" that Lionel Trilling has so admirably provided in his early essay on *Lolita*, entitled "The Last Lover." Trilling begins by rejecting some of the more common ideas about the novel. It is not, he says, a psychological study, a satire of America, a work of moral subversion, nor does it shock the reader for shock's sake. Nabokov intended to write a love story; and to fulfill this objective, he had to write about perverted love.

Here Trilling's argument is based on a sophisticated

use of ideas drawn from Denis de Rougement's classic study, *Love in the Western World*. De Rougement observed that the courtly love tradition of the Middle Ages set down as "a perfectly obvious doctrine" the notion that husband and wife cannot be lovers. "The reason was," says Trilling summarizing de Rougement, "that theirs was a practical and contractual relationship, having reference to estates and progeny . . . not a relationship of the heart. . . ."[2] In later social developments, the middle classes finally demanded love as well as the practical elements within marriage. Yet, as Trilling puts it, modern marriage aspires to health, which shows how far away from the passionate suffering of medieval courtly love it really is. The passionate love of the old tradition was unhealthy, illicit, and scandalous. Now, given modern conditions, if a writer wanted to write about the old kind of love, how could he do it? Faced with this problem, Nabokov could not merely choose to write about adultery, since that is no longer so scandalous; hence, he made Humbert the lover of a twelve-year-old girl.

The reader who fears that this scholarly explanation is the product of Trilling's overactive imagination will find considerable evidence to support Trilling's interpretation within the pages of the novel. Humbert's references to sonnets provide a link to the courtly love tradition, since in its history the sonnet is associated with the troubadours and the courtly ideal of *fin amour*.[3] Humbert frequently tries to justify his passion by citing the saintly parallels of Dante's love for the nine-year-old Beatrice and Petrarch's love for Laura, in spite of the fact that the age differences in those cases were nothing like that in his.

Probably the most apt parallel of the romantic kind, however, is that of Poe's love for his thirteen-year-old cousin, Virginia Clemm, whom he married (though there was some social disapproval) and whom Humbert and

Nabokov assume was the inspiration for Poe's poem, "Annabel Lee." With great descriptive care, Humbert traces his passion for nymphets to the frustration of his first adolescent romance on the Riviera with a girl named Annabel Leigh. Of course, by introducing the connection with Poe, Nabokov moved the love theme into the darker end of the spectrum. The distance between the love of Dante for Beatrice and that of Poe for Virginia (considered as Humbert insists we consider them, within the context of these writers' works) is the distance between the sacred and the illicit, the divinely inspired and the demonically mad.

Beyond the support provided by these details, there is the fact that—as Trilling points out—like the courtly lady on a pedestal, Lolita "remains perpetually the cruel mistress, even after her lover has won physical possession."[4] Perhaps the most conclusive demonstration that Humbert's love is genuine comes near the story's end, when he begs his faded nymphet to leave her husband and come back to him, even though she is no longer at all the sex object he once had worshiped and enjoyed.

There can be no doubt that Lolita was a sex object to Humbert Humbert; but though the label may be a convenient shorthand, the facile application of such an expression tends to impoverish rather than to enrich our understanding of the subject. Those who find Trilling's analysis too literary and historical can turn for help to a branch of contemporary psychological theory, the psychology of object relations. Though he does not discuss Nabokov, Ernest Becker's ingenious articulation of this theory in an essay called "Everyman as Pervert" provides a complementary explanation of Humbert Humbert's behavior.[5] Less subjective than Trilling's, this approach may seem also less imaginative, but only because its assumptions are closer to those of modern behaviorism. Behind this theory lies the old empirical notion, *esse est percipi*—"to be is to be perceived."[6]

This theory assumes that man is an energy-converting organism, for whom to live means to move forward in relation to the objects of the world. What makes an object meaningful is our ability to behave toward it. To lack meaning is, therefore, to lack dependable behavior patterns with respect to objects. The richer the world of objects with which we have dependable patterns of behavior, the more meaningful our lives. The definition of a fetishist (and Becker takes fetishism as a basic component of all "abnormal" behavior) that follows from such a theory is that of a person who responds to partial objects. The male heterosexual fetishist may respond, for example, to a woman's shoe, but not to the whole woman. A healthy subject is thus defined, according to this theory, as one whose life is rich in dependable behavior patterns with many whole objects; and an unhealthy subject, as one whose life is poor in dependable behavior patterns, that is, who behaves dependably toward relatively few objects and toward partial objects.

Anyone consulting his own experience will readily conclude with Becker that no one can respond to all the objects of his world, nor can one avoid responding at least sometime even to the most meaningful objects as partial objects. Hence mature and immature object relations, mature and immature behavior are a matter of degree and not of kind. Becker argues further that not only are we all fetishists to some degree, but also that fetishistic behavior is a cultural imperative. In fact almost all of man's cultural life, according to him, takes place on a fetishistic level. We are taught to attach ourselves to particular objects. "The mission of both science and art," he says, "as the highest of human strivings, is to create new objects and to reveal facets of old objects that we did not know existed."[7]

Brilliant as it is, we are not interested here so much in Becker's indictment of all mankind as perverts, as in understanding one particular pervert's behavior. Becker's theory also explains the strange connection between Humbert Humbert's genius and his pervertedness. Living a life relatively poor in objects and yet still possessing as great a potential for behavior toward objects as anyone else, the fetishist is caught between his poverty, on the one hand, and his native ingenuity, on the other:

The fetishist . . . being limited in behavior . . . is tasked to create *an extra charge of life-enhancing meaning in a more limited area* than is necessary for the rest of us. That is to say, he must fix on some perceptual detail, and derive the *full justification for drawing himself to the object* from this very narrow focalization. It is this very resourcefulness that appears to the outsider as "abnormal."[8]

There can be no more apt description of Humbert Humbert's behavior than Becker's general analysis of the fetishist. In love in the true romantic sense elaborated by Trilling and pursuing his love object with all the ingenuity of the fetishist, Humbert Humbert becomes the genius-artist in whom Nabokov's passion for words finds its fullest expression. Humbert's fetishism is the vehicle that can give the greatest latitude to Nabokov's romance with language.

Trilling's hypothesis of Humbert Humbert as the "last lover" helps us to appreciate *Lolita* as a fable of romantic love, while Becker's theory of fetishism helps us to appreciate the novel's obsessive tone. *Lolita* is not—as John Ray claims in the foreword—the confession of "a white widowed male." It is rather Humbert Humbert's

literary creation, a work of art written with such infectious
and compelling fervor as to become a sustained verbal
conjuring act. All the overlays of the humorous, the
comic, the bizarre, and the grotesque cannot disguise the
fact that at a fundamental level it is a serious story of
love.

Awaiting trial for the death of Clare Quilty, Humbert Humbert has nothing else to do but cherish Lolita's
name as he had cherished her body. One need look no
further than the opening paragraphs for an example of
Humbert's verbal fetishism:

Lolita, light of my life, fire of my loins. My sin, my soul,
Lo-lee-ta: the tip of the tongue taking a trip of three steps
down the palate to tap, at three, on the teeth. Lo. Lee. Ta.

She was Lo, plain Lo, in the morning, standing four
feet ten in one sock. She was Lola in slacks. She was Dolly
at school. She was Dolores on the dotted line. But in my
arms she was always Lolita.

The opening lines are a rhythmic caress. Around her
name, with its sacred syllables, he weaves the story of his
love for her.

Through the genius of Nabokov's style, these opening paragraphs become a microcosm of the basic conflict
of the novel as a whole. The first paragraph is lyrical,
evocative, and incantatory. By making a lyric out of
Lolita's name, Humbert flourishes his verbal talents and
establishes himself as a poet, as an artist capable of
detecting and defining the elusive grace of a nymphet.
Sitting ignominiously in jail, he proudly asserts his creative authority at the outset; and feeling secure that he has
done so, he then flippantly remarks, "You can always
count on a murderer for a fancy prose style."

Writing his story in retrospect, Humbert outlines in
the first two paragraphs the essential duality of what

Lolita was for him. In paragraph one, she is conjured up
as he wished to view her, as an object of beauty, as a
poem and even as an erotic fetish. In paragraph two,
which modulates noticeably from the rhythmic fervor of
paragraph one, he reluctantly acknowledges Lolita's existence as a real person, naming her various roles in the
ordinary world. While granting her existence in those
other roles, however, he returns at the end to the primacy
of her role in his love dream. Part One of the novel traces
his deliciously frenzied efforts to draw Lolita out of the
incomparably less interesting or pleasing real world and
to contain her as long as possible inside the magic circle
of his fantasy.

In Humbert's strategies to possess Lolita, the novel
reflects Nabokov's special passion for games and symmetry. Humbert presents his story as if it were a cosmic
chess match in which he pits his cleverness against that
of Fate. Taking a hint from a name in the list of Lolita's
Ramsdale classmates, Humbert dubs his adversary "Aubrey McFate." Though McFate tantalizes Humbert with
alternatingly cooperative and frustrating moves, Humbert
wins—at least in Part One.

When he has settled in at Ramsdale with Charlotte
and Lolita Haze, Humbert's mind continually projects
erotic fantasies. Even the most innocent activities, actual
or planned, stimulate his imagination. When on one occasion, Charlotte, with her own amorous eye on the handsome boarder, plans a picnic at Our Glass Lake (as
Humbert at first hears the name), Humbert begins to
conjure up the lakeside setting in which he will at last
possess Lolita. But a series of successive misbehaviors on
Lolita's part causes a series of postponements of the
outing and frustrates Humbert. He starts to fear that not
even the real picnic will come off, much less the imagined
feast, and he speaks of the teasing expectation as Aubrey

McFate's "Mirage of the Lake." That Our Glass Lake turns out to be Hourglass Lake is only one of many hints of McFate's hostility.

It is during the days when Humbert Humbert is held by McFate in this state of suspense about the "Mirage of the Lake" that his first sexual contact with Lolita occurs. Instead of a moment of gross animality, it is a moment of rhythm and poetry. What's more—by a miracle of art and artifice—Lolita's innocence is preserved. After all the temptings and thwartings of McFate, Humbert has his chance: "I knew exactly what I wanted to do, and how to do it, without impinging on a child's chastity; after all, I had had *some* experience in my life of pederosis; had visually possessed dappled nymphets in parks; had wedged my wary and bestial way into the hottest, most crowded corner of a city bus full of straphanging school children."

One Sunday morning while Humbert is sitting on the sofa in the Haze living room in his pajamas and "purple silk dressing gown," Lolita enters tossing "a beautiful, banal, Eden-red-apple" and pops herself down beside him. While Lolita's attention is absorbed by their playful competition for the apple and for the magazine Humbert pretends to be reading, his imagination fixes on the extraordinary opportunity offered by Lolita's casually extending her legs across his lap. Mesmerizing his prey by bouncing her legs up and down on his lap and by singing his garbled version of a currently popular song, Humbert manipulates the friction so that he can finally crush "out against her left buttock the last throb of the longest ecstasy man or monster had ever known." Humbert's sexual control is sufficiently strong so that before the final release arrives, he can "slow down in order to prolong the glow."

This scene, which must have indeed been one of

those that first gave potential publishers pause, is a triumph of descriptive power. Just as Humbert Humbert synchronizes a number of simultaneous activities—with the apple, the magazine, Lolita's legs, his song—in order to achieve a moment of bliss, Nabokov himself has ordered an even fuller and more complex array of motifs and devices in this passage in order to create a startlingly artful set piece. In the shaping of this passage Nabokov must have learned something from James Joyce, who created a similar scene in the "Nausicaa" episode of *Ulysses*. There Leopold Bloom masturbates unobtrusively on the beach while watching the flirtatious Gerty McDowell. Joyce synchronized Bloom's sexual release with a fireworks display. Though he has strenuously denied the influence of Joyce and most other writers on his work, Nabokov has at least mentioned this famous scene in *Ulysses* as one whose artistry he admires.[9]

Yet whatever likenesses of substance and technique may exist, the effect of Humbert's manipulation of Lolita is entirely different from the effect of Leopold Bloom's fantasy. What Humbert achieves through his "secret system of tactile correspondence between beast and beauty" is not merely sexual release, but the successful encapsulation of Lolita within his idealized and romantic fantasy world: "Lolita had been safely solipsized." That is to say, he has used Lolita in his private and subjective way for his own pleasure—and presumably without her knowledge or cooporation. In the grand design of the whole, this episode is an early battle Humbert Humbert wins in a war that he must finally lose.

This scene in the living room at 342 Lawn Street, Ramsdale, gives Humbert his first success in grounding his fantasies in reality or in raising reality to the level of his fantasy. The culmination of this process takes place late in Part One. With the sudden death of Charlotte,

Humbert must report the sad news to Lolita, who is away at the time at Camp Q. Ironically, Lolita's stay at the camp had been arranged by her mother so that the just married Charlotte and Humbert could enjoy a quiet honeymoon at home without Lolita's presence. Uppermost, of course, in Humbert's mind is not the responsibility of telling the child about her mother's death, but a mad, half-formed scheme to get her alone.

Even with this mad scheme working in his brain, Humbert is still sensitive to the problem of preserving Lolita's morals, if not her virginity. Even though his morality is considerably looser than that of most men, he strives to guard against a callous treatment of his prey: "I was still firmly resolved to pursue my policy of sparing her purity by operating only in the stealth of night, only upon a completely anesthetized little nude."

McFate seems to cooperate as Humbert takes Lolita away from Camp Q on the pretext that her mother is ill and in a hospital in distant Lepingville. They must drive to visit her by way of the secluded town of Briceland, where Humbert expects to find his first night of perfect bliss. McFate even seems to cooperate by giving an appropriately symbolic name, The Enchanted Hunters, to the inn in which they will spend their first night together. Thinking also of the sleeping pills he has brought with him to insure the preservation of Lolita's morals, he reflects on the symbolic appropriateness of their situation: "Was he not a very Enchanted Hunter as he deliberated over his boxful of magic ammunition?" That their room number, 342, turns out to be the same as their Ramsdale house number seems to Humbert proof that McFate is smiling on his plans.

In room 342 of The Enchanted Hunters, as before in the living room on 342 Lawn Street, Humbert Humbert strives to "solipsize" Lolita. After giving her the sleeping pills, and wandering about the hotel while they take effect, Humbert returns to what he calls the "hermetic seclusion" of their bedroom. There he and the surprisingly wide-awake Lolita become lovers.

It may seem peculiar that a writer who claims, as Nabokov does, to be "Philosophically . . . an indivisible monist" should have produced a masterpiece that is structured on multiple and complex dualities.[10] Many of the dualities of *Lolita* are obvious: Humbert the man versus Humbert the artist, Humbert the man versus Humbert the beast, erotic and poetic fantasy versus prosaic reality. But the dualism is an ingrained quality of the style and structure of the novel as well.

In this play of dualities, the perspective afforded by the first-person point of view is by no means the least important device of contrast. Two Humberts are present on every page of *Lolita*: the Humbert who actually experiences the events narrated, always unaware of what will happen next, and the Humbert who has been through it all and writes his story in a wiser retrospect. Most of the time he is so enthusiastically caught up in the pleasure of re-creating the past that the Humbert pictured as living through the narrated moment seems to dominate. But underneath the old Humbert's excitement, the wiser Humbert's objectivity can be seen from time to time. Even in the midst of recounting his thrilled anticipation of what he would experience in Room 342, the later Humbert knows he "should have understood . . . that nothing but pain and horror would result from the expected rapture." Lost in his own fantasy world, Humbert sees only gradually that Lolita is no heroine in a courtly love romance, but merely an eager teen-aged experimenter, who has already made a few trial runs with a boy at Camp Q.

Part One closes with Humbert's blank announcement

to Lolita that her mother is dead and with his poignant observation that it is the child's simple need for love that brings Lolita to his bed the next night. "You see," Humbert observes, "she had absolutely nowhere else to go."

Part Two recounts Humbert's valiant, but futile efforts to preserve his captured dream. His first strategy is to repeat the episode of The Enchanted Hunters hotel room by taking Lolita on a cross-country auto trip. As Humbert describes it, their "tour was a hard, twisted, teleological growth, whose sole *raison d'etre* was to keep my companion in passable humor from kiss to kiss." His ingenuity in keeping her in passable humor is both impressively imaginative and pathetically desparate:

Every morning during our yearlong travels I had to devise some expectation, some special point in space and time for her to look forward to, for her to survive till bedtime. Otherwise, deprived of a shaping and sustaining purpose, the skeleton of her day sagged and collapsed. . . . By putting the geography of the United States in motion, I did my best for hours on end to give her the impression of "going places," of rolling on to some definite destination, to some unusual delight.

Nevertheless, the relationship begins to falter. The second phase of the dream's dissolution begins when Humbert decides that an improvement in their relationship might come "with a fixed domicile and a routine schoolgirl's day." They settle in Beardsley in a house, which, though some four hundred miles from Ramsdale, nevertheless reminds Humbert vaguely of the house where he first saw Lolita. He is aware that the dangers of discovery are much greater when they move back into the real world of ordinary domestic and social life. He must be on his guard. Just as Part One traces Humbert's mounting anticipation of pleasure, Part Two traces his growing anxiety at the possibility of losing Lolita. He begins to imagine rivals, only to find shortly that a real one does exist.

Humbert is highly amused by Lolita's so-called progressive girls' school, whose headmistress could hardly be expected to guess the degree of liberality existing between Lolita and her distinguished-looking stepfather. But the Beardsley school has the last laugh. Its program of extra-curricular activities is indirectly responsible for Humbert's betrayal. The once obliging McFate now plays Humbert a dirty trick. Grasping at the opportunity to get out from under Humbert's jealous eye, Lolita agrees to take part in a school play. Humbert fears that Lolita's growing restiveness is verging on rebellion. They are caught up in a subtle struggle of wills so strong that he decides the situation is too difficult to handle at Beardsley. They pack their bags to begin another long auto trip, but this time Humbert's worst fears are borne out as he begins to realize they are being followed.

Much later, the doleful Humbert learns that Lolita, chafing increasingly under his burdensome possessiveness, has actually conspired with someone else to free her: "By permitting Lolita to study acting I had, fond fool, suffered her to cultivate deceit." Under the strain of travel, she comes down with a virus and must go to a hospital in the western town of Elphinstone. It is here that the story's reversal takes place. Secretly Lolita conspires to run away with a second man. Humbert searches for her frenziedly all over the face of America, in "342 hotels, motels, and tourist homes." The romance quest of Part One becomes a quest for the lost Lolita and for the identity of her abductor in Part Two.

As in the rest of Nabokov's fiction, the theme of the quest for identity turns ironic. Although Humbert finds out who his rival is only very late in the story, there were dozens of clues strewn along the way. The unsuspecting reader is not likely to have picked up those clues either, and thus shares Humbert's blindness and his consequent self-reproach.

The rival, Clare Quilty, can be traced to the very beginning of Humbert's acquaintance with Lolita. It was Quilty who had posed in the Dromes cigarette ad that Lolita had put up on her bedroom wall beside another ad picturing a man whom she thought resembled Humbert. It was Quilty who had eyed Lolita with interest at The Enchanted Hunters Inn and who is already connected with Ramsdale because his uncle, Dr. Quilty, is the local dentist. The same Quilty is also the famous playwright who wrote the work in which Lolita was to have starred at the Beardsley school. Calling his play "The Enchanted Hunters," Quilty mocks the unwitting Humbert's blissful experience in the inn. Although Humbert took her away from Beardsley before the performance, Lolita had met Quilty, who was invited to Beardsley to see how the production of his play was progressing.

Humbert's motive for murdering Quilty is simple: he wanted to avenge the loss of Lolita. But the moral issues—so complex to begin with—are considerably complicated by Quilty's characterization. Against Humbert's perverted but idealistic love, Nabokov sets Quilty's equally perverted but obscene lust. Being impotent, Quilty cannot achieve carnal satisfaction with Lolita. What he wants from her seems even less savory than what Humbert wanted. Promising her a part in a movie based on one of his plays, Quilty takes her to a borrowed dude ranch. Lolita is rather easily entranced by the famous Quilty, but even so, she refuses to do the things he asks. Five years later, Mrs. Dolly Schiller explains to the visiting Humbert what Quilty had in mind: ". . . he had two girls and two boys, and three or four men, and the idea was for all of us to tangle in the nude while an old woman took movie pictures."

For all Humbert's protestations to the contrary, dramatist Quilty's obscene and voyeuristic art may not appear to the reader so very different from poet Humbert's fantasies. How sordid would Humbert's dreams appear if photographed in all their explicit detail? How repugnant might they appear without the poetry of his narrative account? Through many descriptive details Nabokov tries to suggest that Clare Quilty's pathetic perverseness is merely an uglier version of Humbert's own. This is one more way in which the novel turns back on itself. Almost in spite of Humbert's wishes, the rhythms and revelations of Part Two reestablish a more realistic view of his love story.

As if to illuminate the novel's complex thematic counterpoint in an explicitly structural way, Nabokov framed Humbert's story between a foreword by John Ray, a fictitious expert on "morbid states and perversions," and a postscript by Nabokov himself, an expert on "aesthetic bliss." Nabokov seems to have added the postscript merely to counteract the foreword (and the reading public's criticism), for Ray takes a moral and didactic view of the story and Nabokov, a purely aesthetic view.[11]

Yet the relevance of this frame is much more complex, for both essays have an organic connection with the structure of the novel itself. The extrinsic duality of the foreword and postscript mirrors the intrinsic duality of the two parts of the novel proper. Part One follows Humbert Humbert through to the culminating moment of his bliss as he possesses Lolita for the first time at The Enchanted Hunters Hotel. Part Two traces the loss of that bliss, the dissolution of Humbert's impossible dream through the intervention of Clare Quilty, who had created the play called "Enchanted Hunters," and on to the ultimate tragedy. In Part One Nabokov succeeds in gaining the reader's perhaps unwilling sympathy for Humbert Humbert as he climbs inside his fantasy world, madly wishing to live with his nymphet forever. Having treated his reader to this aesthetic but morally anesthetic blandishment, Nabokov in Part Two reveals to both Humbert and the reader the sad and pathetic truth.

Thus, *Lolita* becomes the consummate example of Nabokov's passion for symmetry, as the foreword balances the aestheticism that dominates Part One, while the postscript balances the moralism of Part Two. In all this brilliant juggling of contradictory values, Nabokov's genius has allowed both sides to win. At last, both the reader and Humbert have had their bliss, even if reality has overtaken them both once again.

5

*Hero
of the People:
Ping-pong Pnin*

*P*nin is as finely constructed as *Lolita* and has a similarly pseudo-biographical thrust. Ostensibly the novel is an account of the life and times of Timofey Pnin, the bumbling but good-natured professor of Russian at Waindell College, located somewhere northwest of Albany, New York. Under this surface, however, Nabokov developed with a special twist his favorite complex of themes—life as a struggle with fate, the gamelike quality of the struggle, the function of the imagination in the game. In typical Nabokovian fashion, the complex of themes drives the novel toward a magic resolution, one less ghostly and evasive than that in *Sebastian Knight* and more elementally optimistic than that in *Lolita*. At the end of *Pnin*, the reader knows more certainly than in *Sebastian Knight* where he is and what has happened, and he may be more encouraged about life than he was after reading *Lolita*. Another touch of artistry makes *Pnin* a masterpiece: the warmth of Nabokov's treatment of his title character. Timofey Pnin is probably the most genuinely endearing figure in all of Nabokov's fiction.

The art of this work incorporates to the highest degree three of Navokov's major talents. The first is the talent for condensed verbal portraiture. The picture of Pnin is economical, yet as full as life itself. The second is the talent for sustaining and then, after gradual preparation, finally integrating all the story's elements into a grand design. *Pnin* moves to a conclusion as surprising as that of *Sebastian Knight*, but a more realistic one. The reader is compelled to admire the control required for the novel's fateful resolution. The third talent is the ingenious handling of point of view. Again, as in *Sebastian Knight*, the narrator is not a transparent medium through whom the story is transmitted, but an actor in the story whose role turns out to be crucial.

Up to a point, Pnin's life parallels in broad outline

that of Nabokov. He was born in the late 1890s in Saint Petersburg and was part of the exodus of Russian liberals and intellectuals who left their country at the time of the revolution. He obtained a degree at a European university (Nabokov's was from Cambridge, Pnin's from Prague), before joining the circle of Russian émigrés in Paris. He emigrated to the United States just before the Nazi occupation of France, later became an American citizen, and settled as a professor at an Eastern college, where he lived the quiet life of academic routine: chats with students, visits to the library, occasional excursions to deliver out-of-town lectures.

Yet here the parallel ends. In his many peregrinations, Nabokov seems always to have been comforted by the presence of his wife and son. Pnin, divorced and very much alone, passes his years in Waindell, moving from one rented room to another in search of a comfort that always eludes him. Moreover, judging from the testimonies of his former students and colleagues, Nabokov's academic career was quite successful. No matter how endearing he may be, Pnin's success at Waindell is dubious. Nabokov's teaching career ended only with the fame and financial independence that came with the publication of *Lolita*. Pnin's career at Waindell terminates with his abrupt departure at midsemester.

In a characteristic twist, Nabokov concluded the novel by shifting the focus onto the narrator, whose pivotal role in Pnin's life is at last clarified. Faced with the imminent loss of his present status and knowing that the narrator will become the principal Slavist the following semester, Pnin suddenly abandons Waindell in the middle of the academic year, rejecting the narrator's friendly overtures. On the February day when the narrator visits the college, which he is to join the next fall, he is witness to Pnin's departure from town. What Pnin preserves by this eccentric behavior turns out to be the point of the tale, and to understand what he preserves, we must examine other details of the story.

The present time of the narrative covers only about four and one-half of Pnin's nine years at Waindell (from the fall semester of 1950 to a point early in the spring semester of 1955), but woven into the novel's texture is a full account of Pnin's earlier life. In flashbacks we see Pnin's childhood in Saint Petersburg, where his father was an eye specialist whose practice included such famous patients as Tolstoy. In a series of vignettes, we learn of Dr. Pavel Pnin's pride when Timofey received an A-plus on an algebra examination, of Pnin's youthful interest in drama, and of his first adolescent love affair. These happy pictures are at first carefully balanced and then later overshadowed by depictions of the sadder side of Pnin's life, in particular, his marriage in Paris to the aspiring poet and medical student, Liza Bogolepov, and that marriage's painful consequences.

The function of these flashbacks is complex. At the simplest level they serve to provide the reader with necessary details about Pnin's past. But they have more sophisticated uses. First, in the manner of Proust (whose name he has frequently mentioned in his novels), Nabokov implies that the past shapes the present and in fact burdens it. Second, in Nabokov's particular interpretation, past episodes in the life of Pnin are depicted as a series of moves in a game with fate. Such a use of flashbacks lends a special depth to this relatively brief novel. Throughout the story the reader is continually sensitized to the play between the present and the past and a similar play between the surface events of life and the more important game with fate that lies behind them.

Occasionally the novel veers in the direction of farce, with Pnin in the role of the middle-aged European profes-

sor whose zany struggle to accommodate to his new
American environment provides humor. At other times it
moves in the direction of satire, as in the not-so-gentle
fun poked at Pnin's colleagues. Instead of surrounding
them with the warmth he gave to Pnin's portrait, Nabokov handled them with a cooler touch. The satirical mode
is never dominant because the story is Pnin's and no one
else's. The farce is purposely controlled by the narrator to
prevent the reader from settling into an automatic
response.

Pnin, it should be particularly stressed, was anything but
the type of that good-natured German platitude of the last
century, *der zerstreute Professor.* On the contrary, he was
perhaps too wary, too persistently on the lookout for
diabolical pitfalls, too painfully on the alert lest his erratic
surroundings (unpredictable America) inveigle him into
some bit of preposterous oversight. It was the world that
was absent-minded and it was Pnin whose business it was
to set it straight.

Pnin is the very antithesis of the absent-minded professor who gives no heed to the realities around him, for
Pnin is always on guard against life's "diabolical pitfalls." His wariness may represent, as the narrator suggests, a comic overreaction; but as the reader gradually
accumulates a total impression of Pnin's losses and sorrows, he comes to respect and appreciate Pnin's wariness.

The burden of Pnin's sadness is carried into the
present time of the narrative most pointedly with the
appearance of his former wife. In one of the novel's most
emotional moments, Pnin receives a visit from Liza. As
always she abuses his kindness, for she has come once
again to exploit Pnin's generosity. Her present husband,
Dr. Eric Wind, shows no affection to their artistically
inclined son, Victor. She has come to ask baldly if Pnin

will occasionally send some pocket money to the boy at his boarding school, or—in other words—father the boy whose real father neglects him. Although he obliges, Pnin is nevertheless pained by Liza's callousness, and in a moment of despair cries out: "I haf nofing left, nofing, nofing!" On another occasion, aware that both his ex-wife and her husband are practicing psychiatrists, Pnin seriously asks: "Why not leave their private sorrows to people? Is sorrow not, one asks, the only thing in the world people really possess?"

Since Pnin is a version of the hero as victim, the novel implicitly asks, by whom is he victimized? The answer is, in part, that all men victimize each other, intentionally or not. This is what happens with the genial Dr. Hagen, to whose good graces Pnin owes his position at Waindell. Left unexpectedly without the support of Dr. Hagen, who takes a job at another college, Pnin seems at first helpless. In part Pnin is victimized by himself, as the narrator suggests. Pnin's exaggerated prudence causes him as much trouble as a lack of caution would. Yet fundamentally it is neither the heartless ex-wife, nor the genial friend, nor even Pnin himself who is responsible for his suffering. That responsibility belongs ultimately to an inscrutable fate that merely uses people and things as agents.

In the novel's opening pages, Nabokov makes fun—but serious fun—of Pnin's efforts to counter fate's troublesome gambits. Pnin is on a train that he thinks is taking him to Cremona, where he will deliver a lecture to a local women's club. He is so inordinately fond of railway schedules that he has failed to notice that the one he is presently using is "five years old and in part obsolete." The stops at Cremona have been discontinued.

There is still more to the situation, for Pnin is caught in a web of circumstances that actually has no end.

Seated on the train, Pnin consciously considers another quandary: shall he keep his lecture manuscript in his suitcase and run the risk of losing it, or shall he keep the manuscript on his person and run the risk of forgetting it when he changes his suit for the evening's activities? Danger lurks, as Pnin is aware, in either choice. The comedy is heightened by the reader's knowledge that poor Pnin, grappling with the problem of the safety of his manuscript, is not even aware of the problem of the train.

In a burlesque sequence of events involving the attempt to switch from train to bus, the loss and recovery of the suitcase and his precious papers, Pnin finally arrives in Cremona on time. But the amusement is tempered at one interval, when Pnin suffers a mild heart seizure, no doubt brought on by the anxiety attending all the confusion. To himself, Pnin denies the seriousness of the attack; but to the reader, the seizure is a reminder that the game with fate is played for keeps: death is, as far as we know, the last move, the one against which there can be no certain countermove.

With the ominous warning that he hates happy endings, the narrator deposits Pnin in Cremona, but not before revealing an essential quality in Pnin's vision of life. At one stage of his journey, Pnin is faced with the unhappy idea of leaving his suitcase behind as he tries to switch from train to bus. Though as things work out, he does not have to leave it behind, the idea is perplexing. But Pnin faces the situation with a mental shrug, as one of life's necessary compromises: "Very well! . . . He would retrieve it on his way back. He had lost, dumped, shed many more valuable things in his day." Such a comment is easily passed over, but it opens a way through the trivial problems at the surface of Pnin's present life into the reservoir of accumulated pain.

Nabokov's overall strategy was gradually to transform the series of rich and evocative flashbacks into a catalog of all the things that Pnin has lost: his country, language, and culture; his parents; his first love, Mira Belochkin, who died in a Nazi concentration camp; his wife, who left him for Dr. Wind; and so forth. Nabokov announces at one point that he is a narrator who dislikes happy endings, thus preparing the reader for the story's ultimate blow: the loss of Pnin's job at Waindell. The poignancy of Pnin's life lies precisely in the fact that, unlike his suitcase, very little of what he has lost has proved retrievable, except in memory. The beauty of Pnin's character lies precisely in his indomitable resilience. He has always managed to look past the problem of the moment, with optimism, even enthusiasm.

In speaking of Pnin I deliberately employ the word "enthusiasm" in its most basic meaning. The English word refers simply to strong feelings. It derives from the Greek word *enthousiazein*, which means to be inspired, to be in a state of religious fervor. Both meanings of the word are appropriate, at least in part, to the characterization of Pnin.

This point of view may explain somewhat why readers who do not like Nabokov's fiction in general still respond positively to *Pnin*. The usual explanation for why this happens is the sheer fun of the novel's farcical descriptions. Yet, as the foregoing discussion implies, there is more pain in Pnin's portrait than pleasure. I would suggest then that these readers who respond sympathetically to Pnin, are reacting to the unusual amount of quite conventional religious imagery in the novel. Though in one passage, Pnin explicitly claims that he is an agnostic, Nabokov infused the story with so much Christian imagery that the reader is tempted to believe that for once Nabokov is writing about the familiar world, a world no longer Christian in the orthodox sense, perhaps, but one with a residue of religious humanism left in it. It is worth noting that in the very passage in which Pnin affirms his agnosticism, the remark results from a friend's observation that Pnin wears a cross on a chain around his neck. Pnin's habitual response to fate's cruel maneuvers seems to be to turn the other cheek; it is as if he volunteers to suffer more.

Although he comes close in this instance to writing a novel in which the hero's behavior reflects not only common values, but almost conventional religious ones, Nabokov limited the religious suggestiveness of his imagery by choosing instead to generalize Pnin's portrait and make him a folk hero. He achieved this by giving Pnin a fondness for proverbs and a repertory of "Russian" gestures. In making Pnin a folk hero rather than a religious hero, Nabokov tended to "normalize" Pnin, that is, to bring him more into the customary range of his characters.

This "normalization," however, is not complete; Pnin remains an unusual character in the Nabokov canon. For, although Nabokov often plays off a folk character, associated with quotidian reality, against an artistic character, committed totally to aesthetic joys, it is unusual for the folk character to come off best, as Pnin does. From time to time, Nabokov throws out hints suggesting that the narrator may finally be revealed as not only the man who succeeds Pnin at Waindell but also his artistic antagonist. Yet Nabokov left this possibility undeveloped, choosing instead to make the relation of artist and folk hero complementary. This new departure is illustrated by the complementary relationship between Pnin and Victor Wind, perhaps the most revealing in the novel.

Contrary to Nabokov's customary practice, the transformation of images into symbols and the lacing of the text with allusions are much less overt in *Pnin*. Characterization and fable seem more important to Nabokov here than symbolic pattern. To put the matter in thematic terms, until the very end, Nabokov seems more concerned with the game fate plays with Pnin than with the game he himself plays with the reader. Yet one subtly elaborated symbolic pattern is central to both character and theme: the water symbolism associated with Pnin's spiritual fathering of Victor Wind.

The friendship of Pnin and Victor actually has little time to develop, but its importance in establishing the depth of Pnin's openness and generosity cannot be over-estimated. Their first actual meeting takes place in 1953, when Pnin invites the fourteen-year-old to Waindell for a visit. But for a long time before, Victor has been involved in one of Pnin's most painful memories. In the 1930s Liza Bogolepov had married Pnin on the rebound after an unhappy affair that had driven her to an almost successful suicide. For her depression, her colleagues in psychiatry prescribed a specific remedy: "Pnin—and a baby at once." After the marriage, Liza's basic wanderlust reasserted itself, and on a December day in 1938, she telephoned Pnin with characteristic brusqueness to say she was leaving him for Dr. Wind. Nabokov describes Pnin's response to the news in a metaphor that links Pnin with life, earth, and growing things, while summing up his generous spirit:

Pnin of course would have given her a divorce as readily as he would his life, with the wet stems cut and a bit of fern, and all of it wrapped up as crisply as at the earth-smelling florist's when the rain makes gray and green mirrors of Easter day; but it transpired that in South America Dr. Wind had a wife with a tortuous mind and a phony passport, who did not wish to be bothered until certain plans of her own took shape.

Shortly thereafter, in the face of the war, Pnin made plans to emigrate to America, only to become the victim of a cruel ruse. Liza, pregnant, suddenly returned to Pnin, announcing that her affair with Wind was over and that she was now ready to settle down. Pnin, in what the narrator calls probably the "happiest" days of his life, took Liza back and was "not only ready" but "passionately" eager to adopt the child. But as they traveled to America, Pnin was accosted on the ship by Wind, who revealed that Liza had returned to her husband only to make her own emigration smoother. Once they reached the States, Liza and Wind departed together, leaving Pnin to start his American life again in loneliness. Thus, the boy Liza asks Pnin to "adopt" in 1953 is the same one Pnin was earlier so eager to adopt.

Liza's request is brazen and cruel, and Nabokov deliberately associated her brittleness and selfishness with her work in psychiatry. When she visits Pnin at Waindell, it seems that time has brought painful changes to her just as it has to him. She and Dr. Wind are not happy; she has taken a new lover; and Dr. Wind has always disliked their child. Needing Pnin's help, Liza jokingly refers to the trick she and Wind played on him. Dr. Wind says, as she explains, that "he is the land father and you, Timofey, are the water father." With this remark Liza initiates a pattern of associated images in the text by which Nabokov contrasted the humanity of Pnin with the shallowness not only of the Winds but also of other characters inclined to laugh at him and treat him callously.

Nabokov used the contrast of land and water in a simple, but effective manner. What Liza means with her joke is that Pnin was allowed to imagine, while they were crossing the Atlantic, that he would be the child's adoptive father, but that as soon as they reached America, Dr. Wind, the child's natural father, took over his role once again. Yet the truth is that Pnin is more of a father to the Winds' son than is Dr. Wind. By associating Pnin with water, Nabokov reinforced his life-giving gentleness, the softness that makes him seem at times too good for this world. By associating the image of land with Dr. Wind, he emphasized Wind's worldly and inhuman toughness.

So that the point would not be lost, Nabokov extended the symbolic suggestiveness of Pnin's role as "the water father." Throughout Liza's visit, the narrator emphasizes Pnin's continuing vulnerability to her. He feels a lingering desire to have her back, even though he is conscious of her faults:

He saw her off and walked back through the park. To hold her, to keep her—just as she was—with her cruelty, with her vulgarity, with her blinding blue eyes, with her miserable poetry, with her fat feet, with her impure, dry, sordid, infantile soul. All of a sudden he thought: If people are reunited in Heaven (I don't believe it but suppose), then how shall I stop it from creeping upon me, over me, that shriveled, helpless, lame thing, her soul? But this is the earth, and I am, curiously enough, alive, and there is something in me and in life—

As the last line indicates, Pnin's spirit is still able—at least in this life—to shake itself free from depression. After each bout with fate he turns hopefully toward life. One such turn is dramatized by an encounter with nature that immediately follows Liza's visit: as he is walking back home through the park, Pnin's melancholy, yet life-affirming reverie is suddenly "interrupted by an urgent request." Noticing a gray squirrel that seems to be begging for help at a water fountain, Pnin turns on the water for him.

Pnin understood and after some fumbling he found what had to be pressed for the necessary results. Eying him with contempt, the thirsty rodent forthwith began to sample the stocky sparkling pillar of water, and went on drinking for a considerable time. "She has fever, perhaps," thought Pnin, weeping quietly and freely, and all the time politely pressing the contraption down while trying not to meet the unpleasant eye fixed on him. Its thirst quenched, the squirrel departed without the least sign of gratitude.

What at first seems but a further example of Pnin's excessively sentimental nature is enlarged by Nabokov's artistry. In the close juxtaposition of the painful visit with the supplicant Liza and the encounter with the contemptuous and ungrateful squirrel, Nabokov reveals both the depth of Pnin's passion and the power of his resilience. Pnin finds solace in earth and nature.

Acknowledging at some level the significance of his role as "the water father," Pnin soon after enters into a correspondence with Victor and asks him to visit Waindell. Pnin's invitation to Victor is sent on the back of an educational series postcard. With odd appropriateness, that postcard illustrates the species of squirrel Pnin met with in the park. Always the teacher, Pnin says here more than he knows.

So spontaneous is the sympathy between Pnin and Victor that the reader familiar with Nabokov's fictional games is prodded to reexamine the earlier details in the hope of learning that Victor might actually be Pnin's son. Such a discovery would satisfy one's taste for literary detective work, and, more important, it would ease the weight of Pnin's loneliness.

Yet there is no such relief, for Pnin and Victor are bound by a spiritual sympathy, not a tie of blood. The folk hero is the spiritual father of the novel's artist figure. Instead of the usual struggle of an artist hero with a hyper-refined sensibility against the bourgeois morality and cloddish ways of the common man, Nabokov here depicted the alliance of two figures representing reality and imagination against a range of characters represent-

ing various human failings. The range runs from the
Winds, who with their Freudian reductions systematically
rob people of the only thing they truly possess, their sorrows, to Jack Cockerell, chairman of Waindell's English
Department, whose hostile mimicking of Pnin's speech,
gestures, and manner becomes paradoxically a sign of his
fascination with the man he ridicules.

The artist Victor finds a truer parent in the old-fashioned and scholarly but earthbound Pnin than in the
Winds, who remain essentially ignorant and suspicious of
their gifted offspring because his personality eludes their
Rorschach tests. Modern and sophisticated, full of fancy
terminology, social pretensions, and all the marks of success, the Winds are completely lacking in the resources
for the simpler and more natural roles.

Nabokov, of course, did not falsify the picture of
Pnin by suggesting that he is less unhappy or less spiritually hungry than anyone else. But the contrast between
Pnin and the Winds is instructive. Liza had run away
with Dr. Wind originally, she told Pnin, because he
"understood her 'organic ego.' " Later, as their marriage
is foundering and Liza is carrying on a new affair, Dr.
Wind tries to "cure" her. In other words, Liza tries to
satisfy her emotional hunger by turning to a new relationship, just as she had done in leaving Pnin for Wind,
while Wind—who, one supposes, is more "professional"
—believes he can cure her of that hunger. Each represents
a false presumption—Wind, the adequacy of a system (in
this case, Freudian psychiatry) to assuage man's needs;
Liza, the efficacy of the aggressive exercise of the will in
reaching out to wring some solace from life. Pnin suffers
no less than others, but is wiser. He knows that reason
cannot "cure" the hunger and that a succession of relationships cannot satisfy it. One cannot force joy from life.

In several off-hand comments, the narrator implicitly

supports this interpretation. On one occasion, he calls Pnin a "surd" (in mathematics, an irrational number) and thus reminds us of Pnin's wise irrationality. On another occasion, he completely denies the notion that man can escape his sense of separateness by any means whatever: "Man exists only insofar as he is separated from his surroundings," he says, meaning also by "surroundings" other human beings.

Against the novel's presumably knowledgeable characters who cannot draw on their own fund of humanity to sustain them and must grasp at phony systems or at passing objects or persons, Nabokov set his indomitable hero. Pnin is grotesquely funny and quite lonely, but also imaginative, resourceful, and wondrously independent. By carefully interweaving some of Victor's and Pnin's daydreams, Nabokov reinforced both the motif of isolation and the motif of Pnin's parental role. Unhappy with his real father, Victor frequently fantasizes about a "more plausible" one, whom he envisions as king of an eastern European country, caught in a solitary struggle against forces demanding his abdication.

Some of the imagery involved in Victor's fantasy shows up later in a daydream of Pnin's, and though Victor's recurrent fantasy never proceeds to the king's abdication and flight, Nabokov intends us to identify Pnin as the "solus rex" of Victor's fancy. Further, the coincidence of images in Victor's and Pnin's minds may well mean that the most satisfying shared experiences man ever has (at least in this life, as the skeptics Nabokov and Pnin hold) are in the worlds of the imagination.

Though it comes later here than in most of his other novels, Nabokov's gamesmanship ultimately asserts itself in *Pnin*. The game that fate plays with Timofey Pnin is overtaken at last by the game the narrator has all along been playing to a limited but growing degree with the reader. The two games suddenly merge in the narrator's revelation of his role in the story. As much as the unkind Liza Wind or the friendly and well-meaning Dr. Hagen, the narrator too has been an instrument of fate in Pnin's life. Throughout the early chapters, the narrator occasionally hints that he has known Pnin, that they have similar backgrounds and professions. But only in the last chapter does the narrator unmask himself and fill in the details of their acquaintance.

This shift of focus and the consequent change of tone have a dramatic effect. The narrator at last admits his responsibility for some of Pnin's greatest pains, but offers no apology. It was, we learn, the narrator's brief romance with Liza Bogolepov that caused her near sui-cide and the subsequent marriage to Pnin. Twenty-five or thirty years later, it is the narrator who, under the aegis of another department, will become the college's principal Slavist. Because the narrator's invitation to teach at Wain-dell comes from Jack Cockerell, who "considered Pnin a joke," the narrator seems to be at first allied with those unsympathetic to Pnin. Yet such is not the case, for as in the relationship of Humbert Humbert and Clare Quilty and that of V and Sebastian Knight, the reader slowly realizes that Pnin and the narrator are like one another in important ways.

Nabokov thus utilized in *Pnin* one of his most fav-ored methods of characterization: the technique of estab-lishing the nature of his principal characters not solely in terms of descriptions of them as singular individuals, but in terms of comparison and contrast between two charac-ters who are at once alike and yet very different. From the similarities of their backgrounds and their profes-sions, one readily sees that the narrator is a man very much like Pnin, but a man that the world of mortals such as Jack Cockerell can recognize as one of its own and therefore take seriously.

In addition, Nabokov used the narrator's revelation at the end to rescue Pnin's story from two continual threats: the tendency to see Pnin as mawkishly sentimental, on the one hand; and to see him—as Jack Cockerell does—as a joke, on the other. The narrator's intrusions establish him as a calm, reasonable, highly controlled man; but he is, at the same time, able himself to take Pnin quite seriously. The narrator's real function is to bridge the gap between the world of Pnin and the real world, and, most important, to bear witness to Pnin's powerful, if eccentric and mysterious humanity.

As is the custom in academic life, the narrator— before joining the Waindell faculty—visits the college in the spring of 1955 to give a lecture and look over the campus. Since he has been given permission to hire anyone he wants to help him with the Russian courses, the narrator had already extended the olive branch to Pnin and offered him a job. Pnin had returned a polite but firm refusal: "Curtly he wrote that he was through with teaching and would not even bother to wait till the end of the Spring Term." The narrator is surprised, even hurt, by Pnin's response. It seems an oddly irrational, even self-defeating rebuff; but the irrationality of Pnin's abrupt departure is only apparent.

Though the fact is not spelled out in the text, Nabokov leaves the impression that Pnin has over the years pieced together for himself the narrator's role in his life. Only such knowledge could account for Pnin's feeling about the narrator. When Hagen first informs Pnin that the narrator is coming to Waindell and suggests that Pnin will be invited to work under the new man, Pnin is uncharacteristically vociferous in his reply: "Yes, I know him thirty years or more. We are friends, but there is one thing perfectly certain. I will never work under him." By leaving Waindell, Pnin preserves his independence and his dignity. From the lawn of the Cockerell home, the narrator sees Pnin leaving town in his "humble sedan . . . crammed with bundles and suitcases." Instead of breathing a sigh of relief, the narrator makes an impulsive dash to catch Pnin on foot, presumably to renew his offer. Unsuccessful and disappointed, he returns to the Cockerells, now reluctantly anticipating yet another of Jack Cockerell's imitations of Pnin.

In addition to the revelations of the narrator's part in Pnin's life, the ending is something of a surprise in other ways. Conditioned by the images of mortality, in particular by Pnin's several heart attacks, the reader half expects that the novel will conclude with the protagonist's death. Or alternatively, conditioned by Pnin's accumulated sufferings, the reader may at least anticipate a sad ending. These expectations are reversed. Even if Pnin's actions are in some sense a realistic fulfillment of Victor's dream of the king-father's abdication, Pnin is alive and well at the novel's end. And one feels that as he leaves Waindell, Pnin bears away with him all of the world's vitality.

In the end, concentration on the protagonist's elementary nature even solves the puzzle of his explosive-sounding name. Nabokov appropriately gave to Pnin's friends the Clementses (with whom Pnin roomed for a time), some of the novel's most telling words about the protagonist. Early in the novel, Joan Clements jokingly refers to Pnin as a "cracked ping-pong ball." At the story's end, Ping-pong Pnin is not cracked at all. Indeed, his energy and resilience (suggested by his plosive name) appear limitless, for they are drawn not from the realm of Newton's physical laws but from the realm of romance and fable. Late in the novel, Laurence Clements alludes to the real source of Pnin's power: "Our friend employs a nomenclature all his own. His verbal vagaries add a new thrill to life. His mispronunciations are mythopoeic. His slips of the tongue are oracular."

It was Dr. Hagen who had convinced the trustees that Pnin's "disarming, old-fashioned charm" was a "delicate imported article worth paying for in domestic cash." At the end, the narrator bears witness to the wisdom of Hagen's judgment, first in a negative and then in a positive way. First he wonders if Jack Cockerell's excessive mimickery of Pnin has not become "by some poetical vengeance . . . the kind of fatal obsession which substitutes its own victim for that of the initial ridicule"; that is, if Cockerell has not become so obsessed with mimicking Pnin, that he himself has become ridiculous. Shortly thereafter, the narrator describes our final glimpse of Pnin in language that evokes and affirms Pnin's continued vitality:

Then the little sedan boldly swung past the front truck and, free at last, spurted up the shining road, which one could make out narrowing to a thread of gold in the soft mist where hill after hill made beauty of distance, and where there was simply no saying what miracle might happen.

6

The Game
of Worlds:
Pale Fire

Lolita elicits two responses from readers, one moral, the other aesthetic. Those in whom the moral viewpoint predominates object to the sacrifice of Lolita's childhood, even though it makes possible Humbert Humbert's memoir, a memoir that constitutes a brilliant novel. Such readers may well be gratified by Nabokov's humane treatment of Pnin, though Nabokov may still have been temporizing by refusing to give *Pnin* a conclusive ending and by simply leaving the protagonist at large in his absurdly comic, but energetic eccentricity. Others more interested in the aesthetic perspective recognize in the author of *Lolita* a master of form and long to see just how much further he can take his technical daring. These readers find their hopes and expectations fulfilled in *Pale Fire*. Some of Nabokov's most sophisticated critics have declared it to be not only his greatest novel but a masterpiece of twentieth-century fiction. In Mary McCarthy's opinion, *Pale Fire* even gives new hope to the beleaguered novel, a genre that many have felt is no longer a viable literary form:

Pretending to be a curio, it cannot disguise the fact that it is one of the very great works of art of this century, the modern novel that everyone thought was dead and that was only playing possum.[1]

If *Pale Fire* provides evidence for the novel's continued vitality, it does so in an ambiguous manner, not so much by serving as a model for future novels but by revealing the remarkable plasticity of the genre. It is an experimental work, one that defies fiction's conventions.

The novel is in the form of a carefully prepared and scholarly edition of a poem. It is, we are told, a labor of love, undertaken by an editor especially qualified for the job by his close intimacy with the poet and by the influence his friendship had on this, the poet's last and sup-

posedly greatest work. The 999-line poem was written by
John Shade (1898–1959), an American poet whose crag-
gy features and homely metaphysical style are supposed to
remind one of Robert Frost. Shade was shot before finish-
ing his poem; and through the eagerness and hard work
of the editor, Charles Kinbote, it has been published not
long after the poet's death. The foreword (dated October
19, 1959), notes, and index have been prepared by Kinbote, who was the poet's next-door neighbor and colleague
at Wordsmith University.

All this is plausible enough, but the reader does not
proceed far before discovering that the edition is something less than scholarly. The foreword is written in a
nervously meandering style, marked by irrelevant interjec-
tions and obvious proofreading errors. The great haste
and consequent carelessness are the products of the peculiar pressure under which Kinbote has labored. He, the
reader gradually surmises, was never truly intimate with
the poet; but in the few months they were neighbors and
acquaintances, he dreamed up an elaborate fantasy about
his own importance in Shade's life and in the poem
Shade was working on when he died. Because Kinbote
tried to shield the poet from the murderer's bullets, the
widowed Sybil Shade, in a grateful moment, gave Kinbote permission to edit and publish the poem, entitled
"Pale Fire." Though she later changed her mind and
wired Kinbote asking that he at least collaborate with colleagues probably more suited to the task, he ignored the
widow's wishes, and completed the work in hiding at
"Cedarn, Utana," far from "New Wye, Appalachia,"
where he and Shade had lived and worked.

If the foreword suggests to the bewildered reader
that editor Kinbote is not merely under a strain but quite
mad, there is plenty to support such a view. By means of
his lengthy annotations (which along with the foreword

and the index comprise nearly ninety percent of the novel), Kinbote tries to demonstrate that behind the poem's surface lies a subtle meaning that can only be brought out by his skillful and knowledgeable commentary. *Pale Fire* thus becomes a lively parody of scholarly editing, in which the reader is audience to a strange literary struggle between a simple and homely but rather beautiful poem with its own innate meaning and a mad editor who tries to "read into it" a story of his own making.

The poem itself is straightforward and readily intelligible. It is an autobiographical memoir in verse, in which the sixty-one-year-old Shade recounted the salient details of his life—details concerning his parents, both ornithologists, who lived in New Wye and raised him in the house he lived in until his death; the special sensitivity he always possessed, ever since childhood, along with the fainting fits that seemed a part of that sensitivity; his tender feelings for his wife, who was his high-school sweetheart, and for their ugly-duckling daughter, whose death by suicide stimulated his already well-developed tendency toward philosophical speculation; his method of composing poetry; and his views on the larger questions of life, death, and the hereafter.

The poem is direct, coherent, and easily intelligible; yet to understand the novel of which the poem is quantitatively so small a part, the reader must put together the story Kinbote is trying to tell. That story is related in scattered, disjointed, achronological fashion, according to the peculiar associative patterns of Kinbote's mind. Not only are the connections he finds between his story and Shade's poem absurdly tenuous, but the story itself is so bizarre that it further knocks the reader off balance, if he has any left.

Kinbote's narrative is a rich and complex expansion

of Victor Wind's fantasy of the king-father in *Pnin.* In
fact, it has more than enough excitement to outmatch
Victor's juvenile fantasy; yet the king in the case of *Pale
Fire* can father nothing, and his sterility contributes to the
novel's central thematic point. Working at the crossword
puzzle of notes, the reader learns that the forty-four-year-
old Kinbote, recent immigrant from the northern European country called Zembla, and, as of the spring semester
of 1959, teacher of Zemblan at Wordsmith University, is
in actuality the Zemblan king, Charles the Beloved,
deposed in 1958 by a revolution. After months of imprisonment, King Charles, aided principally by Odon (Don-
ald O'Donnell, when he changes his Zemblan name to an
Anglo-Saxon one) and also by many other royalist patri-
ots, escaped from Zembla to the United States, where he
was further helped by Sylvia O'Donnell, Odon's mother
and a trustee of Wordsmith University.

Kinbote-King Charles is a scholarly pederast, whose
life in Zembla was a tangle of homosexual escapades and
court intrigues, the latter largely devoted to getting him
married. He did finally take the beautiful Disa as his
queen, but the marriage was never consummated, thus
there was no heir. The sexually unproductive Charles
channeled his creative urge into another direction (though
he continued to seek pleasure in homosexual liaisons).
Following the family tradition set by his uncle, Conmal,
a "noble paraphrast" famous in Zembla for his translations of Shakespeare (particularly *Timon of Athens,* from
which Shade derived the title of his poem), Charles
became a student of literature. So proficient was his
scholarship that by the age of forty, he had begun to lecture at Onhava University, in his capital city. He taught
in a disguise, since it would have been unseemly for the
reigning monarch to take on such work in his own person.
Thus inured to intrigues and deceptions—all of which

he accepts as the basis of life—and also vocationally prepared, Charles the Beloved is pushed by the revolution
into becoming Charles Kinbote, the professional scholar.

With characteristic whimsy, fate's game works also
to Kinbote's advantage. With the aid of Sylvia O'Donnell,
he not only attains a professorship at Wordsmith, where
his favorite American poet, John Shade, teaches, but also
rents a house next door to Shade's residence. Wildly ego-
centric and self-obsessed, Kinbote is convinced that fate
has brought him into contact with Shade so that the
romance of what Kinbote calls his "glorious misfortunes"
can be recorded for posterity in poetry. Beyond the simple
desire to meet the poet whose work he has long admired
(and even translated into Zemblan) stands Kinbote's
grander motive. During the few months of their acquaintance (from February through July of 1959), while Sybil
Shade is trying to protect her husband from the insistent
intrusions of Kinbote, Kinbote turns voyeur, spying daily
on the Shades' home, at first in search of any opportunity
to convey the facts of his past to Shade and later in search
of any sign that Shade is in fact getting down to the work
of incorporating Kinbote's story into a poem.

Kinbote's interest in "Pale Fire" is thus a result of
his belief that the poem constitutes a brilliant verse chronicle of the history of Zembla, including the tragedy of the
revolution, Charles's dethronement and flight. Having
wrested the manuscript from the momentarily weakened
Sybil, Kinbote discovers that the poem contains little, if
indeed any, of the precious materials he had fed to Shade.
Undaunted, Kinbote nonetheless feverishly searches the
text, word by word, to find even the smallest, vaguest,
most tenuous hint of his story. In the note to 1.42 of
the poem, Kinbote further explains his continued search
in terms of a paranoid delusion of censorship: ". . . we
may conclude that the final text of *Pale Fire* has been

deliberately and drastically drained of every trace of the material I contributed." But he is elated to find "that despite the control exercised upon my poet by a domestic censor [meaning Sybil Shade] and God knows whom else, he [the poet] has given the royal fugitive a refuge in the vaults of the variants he has preserved."

Pale Fire is then essentially a twofold work made up of John Shade's poem and Charles Kinbote's personal narrative. The challenging task for the reader is to decide what true connection there is between the two parts of the novel.

The mere fact that the novel is structured on a duality (poem plus editorial apparatus) does not make it stand out in the Nabokov canon. One of the most prominent metaphors in Nabokov's work is that of the mirror. It includes conveniently both the idea of reflection (the doubling of an image) and that of distortion (the reversal of left and right). But Nabokov was not satisfied with this degree of metaphoric suggestiveness. He also took advantage of the increased complexity involved in placing two mirrors opposite each other. One mirror produces simple reflection and distortion, but two mirrors facing each other at a slight angle produce an infinite series of reflections and distortions.

Sometimes Nabokov used the image of the mirror for local amusement, as in the case of Hermann in *Despair*, who finds his sex life enhanced through the magic of mirrors. Narcissist that he is, he enjoys watching himself make love to his wife in a mirror, and later discovers he can magnify the effect by using two mirrors.

Humbert Humbert achieves a pleasure similar to Hunters Motel. But far more important to any analysis Hermann's in the mirrors of Room 342 of the Enchanted of *Lolita* is the recognition, suggested in chapter four, of the lengths to which Nabokov extended the metaphor.

The idea of two mirrors facing each other is the implicit basis for the structure of the novel as a whole. One can view the first part of *Lolita* as Humbert's successful creation of a dream world in spite of reality's hindrances, and the second part as reality's reassertion of itself and the consequent dissolution of Humbert's dream world. Hence, the structural principle of *Lolita* is that of two perspectives confronting each other, the perspective of dream and that of reality.

The relation between dream and reality is a symbiotic one. Reality serves dream by providing the concrete images from which dream makes its fabrications. Dream serves reality by infusing it with human meaning. If we want to reduce *Lolita* to anything so vague and anti-Nabokovian as a "message," we might say that the story illustrates how life is a drama played out between the real world and the dream world. As we read the novel, we follow Humbert Humbert as he lives through the tensions generated by these mutually needful, but also mutually antagonistic perspectives.

Lolita's structure is indeed sophisticated, but in the testing of form, *Pale Fire* marks a recognizable turning point in Nabokov's career. Here he moved us out of the relatively more safe, if amusing, position between the parallel mirrors and shoved us through the looking glass with Alice. In *Lolita* the structural duality is latent, while in *Pale Fire* it is overt. In *Lolita* the reader is merely expected to follow Humbert Humbert as he plays the game with fate, as he pursues the clues fate has planted to the overall design and meaning of his life. But in *Pale Fire*, the reader himself must get directly involved in the game, for his active participation in making the story meaningful is required.

Stylist that he is, Nabokov has always produced poetic novels, full of metaphors and allusions whose patterns he hopes the reader will trace out. But with *Pale Fire* he exploded the former union of poetry and novel, turned the world of his fiction inside out, and emptied its disjointed contents on the table before us, so to speak—the poetry on one side and the narrative on the other. Upping the ante of his game, Nabokov left the integration of poem and narrative for the reader to manage as best he can, a task made especially teasing since Kinbote has already done such a zany job of it before the reader gets his chance to play.

The reader familiar with Nabokov's earlier works might not be surprised by the structural intricacy of *Pale Fire*. Nevertheless, the novel disarms with the unexpected and becomes a delightfully teasing formal puzzle. Similarly, one might also have anticipated the reappearance of the usual Nabokovian themes, yet *Pale Fire* offers an almost unimaginable freshening and deepening of familiar questions. Of course, the gimcrackery invites—even makes it necessary for—the reader to lose himself in the byways of its magical technique. The sheer delight never fades, but one does eventually move from Nabokov the conjurer (and the question "How did he do it?") to Nabokov the novelist (and "What has he done?").

Novels are about people, not about words or objects, jokes or tricks: and—even by this standard—*Pale Fire* proves to be a novel. Whether Kinbote's perception of reality is right or wrong (and he is most certainly right in some matters, horrendously wrong in others), the core of the book's meaning lies, strangely enough, just where he says it does—in his relationship with John Shade. Whatever statement the novel makes must be gleaned through the implicit contrast or comparison between the principal characters, whose similarities and differences range along a spectral sliding scale from the very gross to the very delicate. In the friendship of Shade and Kinbote, Nabokov explored once again the interconnection (even the mutual need) between dream and reality, art and life.

Because one learns of their relationship only from what the mad Kinbote says about it (John Shade's poem offers *literally* nothing on the subject), one treads on dangerous ground in pretending to describe their friendship in anything like objective terms. But Nabokov wished to make an objective assessment difficult, since—as I have stressed before—he is committed to subjective and personal values. The novel presents once again the story of a man living a difficult life balanced between the extremes of total solipsism and complete capitulation to the freaks and chances of external reality. It both illustrates the pleasures and perils of subjectivity and challenges the reader's judgment. Whether or not his view of the poem is correct, Kinbote's reading is brilliantly inventive, and the reader can thus enjoy it without entirely trusting it.

Kinbote introduces the feeling of extremity in his foreword, implicitly in the strain that shows through his writing, but explicitly in the manner in which he relates his attitude toward the poet and toward the poem itself. In a prefatory note, even the most severe editor might permit himself a mild sentimentality or two, regarding the work, its author, or—more likely—those colleagues and friends who have "made the work possible" through their aid and encouragement. Once the business of defending his editorial procedure is finished, however, Kinbote transforms his foreword into an inordinately romanticized obeisance to Shade, to whom he continually refers in personal terms such as "my dear friend" and "my dear poet." The peculiar fervor of the foreword transmutes John Shade and "Pale Fire" into Kinbote's personal eidolons. The reader who considers the poem immediately after reading the foreword (as is reasonable) must be struck by the contrast. Shade's poem is written in a relatively simple style (deceptively so) ; Kinbote's language is florid and wildly hyperbolic.

Kinbote's description of John Shade's person may serve to illustrate the hyperbole of his style and the general extremity of the foreword:

John Shade's physical appearance was so little in keeping with the harmonies hiving in the man, that one felt inclined to dismiss it as a coarse disguise or passing fashion; for if the fashions of the Romantic Age subtilized a poet's manliness by baring his attractive neck, pruning his profile and reflecting a mountain lake in his oval gaze, present-day bards, owing perhaps to better opportunities of aging, look like gorillas or vultures. My sublime neighbor's face had something about it that might have appealed to the eye, had it been only leonine or Iroquoian; but unfortunately, by combining the two it merely reminded one of a fleshy Hogarthian tippler of indeterminate sex. His misshapen body, that gray mop of abundant hair, the yellow nails of his pudgy fingers, the bags under his lusterless eyes, were only intelligible if regarded as the waste products eliminated from his intrinsic self by the same forces of perfection which purified and chiseled his verse. He was his own cancellation.

Refusing to take Shade simply as a man, Kinbote reads him like a poem, sees in his body and mind an aesthetic design with metaphysical implications. Kinbote describes the simple act of observing Shade as a complex aesthetic response, betraying at the same time his own creative power:

Here he is, I would say to myself, that is his head, containing a brain of a different brand than that of the synthetic jellies preserved in the skulls around him. He is looking from the terrace (of Prof. C.'s house on that March evening) at the distant lake. I am looking at him. I am witnessing a unique physiological phenomenon: John Shade perceiving and transforming the world, taking it in and taking it apart, re-combining its elements in the very process of storing them up so as to produce at some unspecified date an organic miracle, a fusion of image and music, a line of verse.

Kinbote's foreword is more than simply an introduction, or even a defense. It is a verbal rite—something akin to Humbert Humbert's hymn to Lolita's name in the beginning of that novel—by which Kinbote, as priest-king, introduces the reader, as initiate, into the mysteries of his private myth.

To suggest that Kinbote's narrative is creative and that it mythologizes John Shade and his poem may sound much too positive to the unsympathetic reader inclined to view it rather as a parasitic growth feeding on Shade's defenseless poem. Kinbote's narrative is parasitic, but that hardly minimizes its creativity. (In any case, the poem is far from defenseless. It has its own integrity and proves, as Kinbote admits from time to time, remarkably resistant to his efforts to make of it what he will.) The positive aspect of Kinbote's activity must be insisted upon because the urge to create is so vividly present in the power of his style and in the erotic motif threaded closely throughout his part of the book. Kinbote's method of perceiving the world is aesthetic and highly sexual. His style moves easily and frequently from the sensuous to the sensual, from the beautiful to the lascivious.

In his editorial foreword, which has so many other unbusinesslike elements, Kinbote calls attention to the sexual through hints and allusions to his libidinal preferences. Such hints come sometimes in connection with minor issues, as when he complains about the lack of heat in the house he lived in in New Wye. The living room, he says, has

nothing between it and the arctic regions save a sleazy front door without a vestibule—either because the house has been built in midsummer by a naïve settler who could not imagine the kind of winters New Wye had in store for him, or because oldtime gentility required that a chance caller at the open threshold could satisfy himself that nothing unseemly was going on in the parlor.

Not only is this remark sexually suggestive, but it further exemplifies how Kinbote thinks in terms of extremes. The reason for the lack of a vestibule is linked, on the one hand, to naiveté (too little knowledge) and on the other, to suspicion (too much).

Shortly after this passage, Kinbote describes his first private conversation with Shade, whom he had met a few days before surrounded by other faculty members at lunch. They stood outside a classroom building, Shade waiting for Sybil to fetch him in the car, Kinbote lingering for a few precious moments of talk and hoping Sybil would be late so that he himself could drive his neighbor home. Kinbote allows the reader to follow his train of thought here as he looks over "two radiant lads" passing by in front of them, and, shortly afterward, as he thinks of his plans for "a kind of little seminar at home" with "two charming identical twins and another boy, another boy." The repetition of "another boy" may be an example of Kinbote's careless proofreading, or—equally likely —it may be a slip intended to evoke the keenness of his anticipation.

These hints and others that reveal the sexual aspect of Kinbote's specialness, are part of a game of partial self-realization that Kinbote plays with the reader. In the foreword he reports how one day he was alarmed when Dr. Nattochdag, head of his department, called him into his office and announced that a "boy had complained to his adviser." When Kinbote learned the nature of the complaint, that he had criticized the content and the teacher of another course the boy was taking, Kinbote breathed a sigh of relief. On the surface, little more is produced here than some comic fun made of Kinbote's sexual proclivities, yet beyond this, Nabokov purposely associated one side of Kinbote's creative urge (the sexual) with another (the literary). In a fearful moment when he thinks he is going to be chastised (or worse) for giving free expression to his sexual preferences, Kinbote is instead warned against giving free expression to his aesthetic preferences. The reader cannot ignore the fact that the two are closely allied.

Kinbote symbolizes an unusual degree of estrangement. Almost any amount of self-expression is dangerous for him, since he has so much to hide, so many secrets— more even than similar characters like Sebastian Knight or Humbert Humbert. His identity as the deposed King Charles of Zembla must be hidden because of the danger of assassination. Even when he recounts Charles the Beloved's exploits to John Shade, it is in the third person. He cannot freely reveal his sexual inclinations for general social reasons, though, as we learn in the foreword, they are readily deduced by many in New Wye. He is also a vegetarian, which to the community of characters in the novel and also to the reader, is another signal of his aloofness from usual tastes and customs; but we are never allowed to forget that to Kinbote himself these eccentricities are a sign of superiority and purity.

A latter-day Oscar Wilde, Kinbote protects himself from the world at large with a fine wit, but also with a protective snobbery that makes him widely unpopular. For instance, in a skit by some Wordsmith drama students, he was "pictured as a pompous woman hater with a German accent, constantly quoting Housman and nibbling raw carrots." On another occasion, "in the middle of a grocery store," he was accosted by a "ferocious lady," who said: "You are a remarkably disagreeable person. I fail to see how John and Sybil can stand you . . . What's more, you are insane."

Though he registers and reports them (and is doubtless at some level touched by them), Kinbote dismisses these intrusions into his world by a hostile reality. "Let me not pursue the tabulation of nonsense," he says in the foreword, and plunges delightedly into a description of his great friendship with Shade. And here especially the erotic undertone is important:

Whatever was thought, whatever was said, I had my full reward in John's friendship. This friendship was more precious for its tenderness being intentionally concealed, especially when we were not alone, by that gruffness which stems from what can be termed the dignity of the heart.

If one does not perceive the lascivious tone here, one cannot miss it after reading the notes. In one note, for example, Kinbote describes his impulse to visit Shade one day after noticing that Sybil has gone out. On this occasion, he says playfully that he "resembled a lean wary lover taking advantage of a young husband's being alone in the house!"

John Shade's friendship and his art provide a valued refuge for a weary outcast, even though Kinbote's own evidence suggests that Shade could not have attached anywhere near so much importance to that friendship as Kinbote did. Whatever the objective facts, one must be persuaded by Kinbote's rhetoric that the friendship and the poem mean a great deal to him. But there is no way to test the validity of what Kinbote says about his friendship with Shade, for the only account of that friendship we have is his.

We can, however, test the validity of another important assertion Kinbote makes in his foreword:

Let me state that without my notes Shade's text simply has no human reality at all since the human reality of such a poem as his (being too skittish and reticent for an auto-biographical work), with the ommission of many pithy lines carelessly rejected by him, has to depend entirely on the reality of its author and his surroundings, attachments, and so forth, a reality that only my notes can provide.

Nothing could be further from the truth, for "Pale Fire" conjures up the very full "human reality" of John Shade. Kinbote's reading cannot alter, though it may enhance, that reality, in ways that Kinbote himself cannot possibly recognize, though the reader must. Just as *Lolita* is a memorial to love, *Pale Fire* is the record of an attempted seduction. Just as Humbert Humbert, in the very act of possessing Lolita, finds the tables turned on him, when she takes over active control, Charles Kinbote's attempted literary ravishment backfires, for the real humanity of Shade shines through his poem, illuminating all the unreal romance of Charles Kinbote and his life.

Nearly every detail of *Pale Fire* functions precisely to illuminate the likenesses and differences between Kinbote and Shade. One may begin reading the novel with the rather philistine assumption that since all artistic types are sensitive and strange and necessarily self-conscious, Kinbote and Shade are probably a good deal alike. One might further tend to assume that—like V in relation to his brother—Kinbote might wish to emphasize their similarities for the sake of claiming a spiritual closeness that might make his commentary on the poem more convincing.

Creative they both may be; but for the meaning of this novel, the differences of the principal characters are more important than their likenesses. For example, after making the grand claim that his notes give reality to Shade's poem, Kinbote confesses: "To this statement my dear poet would probably not have subscribed, but, for better or worse, it is the commentator who has the last word." A principal difference is more fully aired in one of the notes, when Kinbote recounts at length a conversation in which Shade and he debated philosophical and religious questions concerning death, the afterlife, and God. Kinbote reveals himself to be a high churchman, an orthodox Christian believer who takes the doctrinaire attitude on these issues and who, in fact, feels sorry for the nonbeliever. He even makes a few patronizing thrusts and parries at Shade, though one suspects that it is the beauty of ritual rather than commitment to doctrine on which his faith is founded.

John Shade was as passionately interested in the questions as Kinbote, but he was a realistic skeptic. Following much the same deistic argument as that of the eighteenth-century English poet, Alexander Pope, whom Shade had studied and taught and on whom he had written a book, Shade argued—both in the reported conversation and in the poem itself—that the only genuine evidence for God's existence is not deductive (accepted dogma) but inductive (the design visible in the universe). Shade stopped short of trying to elaborate upon any ideas about God or religious principles from the design he perceived and rested content with tracing its patterns:

> Yes! It sufficed that I in life could find
> Some kind of link-and-bobolink, some kind
> Of correlated pattern in the game,
> Plexed artistry, and something of the same
> Pleasure in it as they who played it found.
>
> It did not matter who they were. No sound,
> No furtive light came from their involute
> Abode, but there they were, aloof and mute,
> Playing a game of worlds, promoting pawns
> To ivory unicorns and ebon fauns;

Kindling a long life here, extinguishing
A short one there; killing a Balkan king;
Causing a chunk of ice formed on a high-
Flying airplane to plummet from the sky
And strike a farmer dead; hiding my keys,
Glasses or pipe. Coordinating these
Events and objects with remote events
And vanished objects. Making ornaments
Of accidents and possibilities.

In John Shade's philosophy the important thing is "not text, but texture"; for through the perception of texture, one sees the world not as "flimsy nonsense, but a web of sense." Paralleling Kinbote's dogmatic Christianity, Shade's religion of design offers its own version of free will. The last thing Shade would have wanted is that everyone perceive the same exact pattern; that would not be beauty, but automatism.

Kinbote identifies by implication the most general difference between himself and Shade when he refers in the notes to the poet's life as "singularly uneventful." Since he had lived and worked all his life in New Wye, resided apparently always in the same house, and as a poet and teacher interested himself almost exclusively in the adventures of the mind, John Shade's outward life had none of the glamour and romance of Charles Kinbote's. Shade was always a down-to-earth man. He lived an ordinary life, and yet by his genius managed to make out of it beautiful poetry. Kinbote's regal and romantic past makes him more of a character in fiction than in the real world. Consequently his attachment to the down-to-earth poet, John Shade, symbolizes his need to breathe somehow the atmosphere of art in order to remain alive. When Kinbote knew him, Shade was old, ugly, and sick with a failing heart that had always threatened death. He had been physically awkward his whole life, and limped in old age. But he accepted his mortality with rough grace, intelligence, and tolerance, writing his poems all the while. Kinbote's and Shade's differing responses to mortality enhance their contrasting portraits. Kinbote is the romantic escapist; Shade, the seeker for universal design.

The characterization of Kinbote and Shade carries the tensions between art and life, imagination and reality that are Nabokov's primary themes. Should the reader allow himself to make the choice between Kinbote and Shade as principal character in *Pale Fire*, as he often feels himself urged to do? Has the very ordinariness of Shade's life made possible his art? Does the fact that Kinbote has lived a life as romantic as a poem mean that he cannot be himself an artist? Still, is there not art in everything Kinbote writes? Is it not, after all, conceivable that Shade has written the whole novel, impersonating a real or imagined madman who harrassed him while he was writing the poem and thus giving free play to his own less-than-ordinary side? Because one can give both affirmative and negative answers to all these questions, one is led to the conclusion that Nabokov was doing what Shade says in his poem the gods are doing—that is, "playing a game of worlds." The novel illustrates not only how reality is mirrored differently in the subjectivity of each person who views it, but how the further mirroring that results from the interplay of minds creates still different views of reality.

Since death ends this play of realities, it is of crucial interest to both Shade and Kinbote. Death is the dominant overt theme both of Shade's poem and Kinbote's narrative, but again their perspectives on the matter are quite different. The novel assumes a strongly allegorical quality when, in an early note, Kinbote confesses that it was his fear of death that actually led him to the obsessive interest in John Shade:

Often, almost nightly, throughout the spring of 1959, I had feared for my life. . . . Everybody knows how given to regicide Zemblans are: two Queens, three Kings, and four-teen Pretenders died violent deaths, strangled, stabbed, poisoned, and drowned in the course of only one century (1700–1800). . . . everything sounded to me like a blood-thirsty prowler. . . . I suppose it was then, on those mas-querading spring nights with the sounds of new life in the trees cruelly mimicking the cracklings of old death in my brain . . . that I got used to consulting the windows of my neighbor's house in the hope for a gleam of comfort. . . .

So preoccupied is Kinbote with the fear of death that he claims in his narrative that John Shade was mistakenly shot by an assassin sent from Zembla to kill him. In an absurdly systematic fashion, he correlates (tracing a pat-tern that does justice to Shade's idea of design) in one of his notes the movements of the supposed assassin—identified by Kinbote as Jakob Gradus, though he appears under many aliases—with the composition of "Pale Fire." On the basis of his talk with the assassin in jail, Kinbote assures us that the plot against him was started in early July, just as Shade's work on the poem was getting under way. Thus, with a mad hindsight, Kinbote perceives the real drama of "Pale Fire" as essentially the question of whether or not John Shade would be able to finish giving King Charles and glorious Zembla a permanent poetic life before the assassin accomplished his work. The impression of Kinbote's madness is only enhanced when the reader learns that everyone else believes the assassin to have been an escapee from jail, who mistakenly killed Shade after confusing him with the absent owner of Kinbote's house, Judge Goldsworth.

Whether the murderer was a revolutionary assassin or a vengeful convict, Shade was a victim of the same apparent nonsense about which he wrote in his poem. Whatever else Kinbote's narrative does, it tries to transform (in a mad version of Shade's own notion) that "flimsy nonsense" into a "web of sense." Aware that he will not be able to escape death forever, Kinbote knows at the end of the book that in the future he will be awaiting "a bigger, more respectable, more competent Gradus." Kinbote is terror-struck by death. John Shade had—as the poem reveals—meditated upon death and lectured on it for the Institute of Preparation for the Hereafter, and had been saddened by it in the suicide of his daughter. Yet the poem is in reality an optimistic summing-up of Shade's life, a testament to his belief in the power of the human imagination. Its tone suggests that he has been "supremely blest" (to borrow the title of Shade's book on Pope, which he himself had borrowed from his subject). Though he dies, he has not been defeated by death, for even if the glow of his own mind has gone out, "Pale Fire" remains, casting its warmth and light. In this connection one ought to add that, though he continues to live after Shade, Kinbote also continues to bear the mark of death.

Pale Fire illustrates a view of life that is remarkably simple, yet endlessly fertile. Life is a "game of worlds" in which there is a limitless multitude of created realities, some (like butterflies and sunsets) the direct products of nature, some (like poems and novels) the indirect products of nature operating through the human mind. Each thing is a world unto itself, with its own pattern, color, consistency, texture. As such, each individual thing—by virtue of its uniqueness, separateness, and concrete particularity—denies and mocks to some degree the reality of all others. Life is thus infinitely full of natural and man-made parodies.

Charles Kinbote, the mad exile from Zembla (which means—according to him—a land of reflections and re-semblers) reports an observation of John Shade on pre-cisely this subject: "Resemblances are the shadows of differences. Different people see different similarities and similar differences." In other words, the question of re-semblances and differences is utterly subjective. The recognition of them is based on the play of lights and shadows, whose angles vary according to a complex of variables involving the perspective of the perceiver and the operations of nature. By proudly preening in its unique-ness, each thing casts shadows on other things, shading or diminishing their light, and being shaded and dimin-ished by their light. In this view, life is a competition of realities, an endless game whose players come from and go to the blackness of oblivion at birth and death.

It is this understanding of life that governed Nabo-kov's choice of a title. Shade offers a clue to what the title means in the context of his poem when he says "No furtive light came from their involute abode."[2] The gods shed no light on what they are doing. In Shade's philoso-phy, which is the same as that governing the work as a whole, each man makes his own light through the per-ception of patterns and designs. Shade thus modestly offers the world his poem as a "pale fire," which casts some light on life. Here, he is saying, is what I have made of it all. In this perspective, Kinbote's innocent (if any-thing he says is) description of Shade as a "fireside poet" becomes, appropriately enough, a metaphysical as well as a physical description. For Shade physics and metaphysics are one and the same. Such is the implication of the now famous opening lines of his poem:

> I was the shadow of the waxwing slain
> By the false azure in the window pane.

At one level, he is talking about a trick of optics; at another, about the play of worlds. His poem begins with the death of the waxwing, which through observation and meditation offers him a chance to make some sense of life. At the end of the novel, Kinbote has become the shadow of the poet slain.

For Kinbote there is another meaning in the title. He finds that the poem is not the "blaze of bliss" for which he had hoped, since it contains only vague hints of his Zemblan chronicle and since the clearest allusions to it appear only in the variants Shade had discarded. Thus, the title is a dual emblem of the realistic modesty of John Shade, on the one hand, and the romantic disappointment of Charles Kinbote, on the other.

The ultimate origin of the title is Shakespeare's *Timon of Athens.* Perhaps most revealing of all is the comparison of the exact lines of the play with the version of them Kinbote gives in his notes. Because he prepared his edition in remote Cedarn, without the aid of a library, he was able to quote the lines only in the roundabout way of Englishing his Uncle Conmal's Zemblan translation. The lines in Shakespeare read as follows:

> I'll example you with thievery;
> The sun's a thief, and with his great attraction
> Robs the vast sea; the moon's an arrant thief,
> And her pale fire she snatches from the sun;
> The sea's a thief, whose liquid surge resolves
> The moon into salt tears; the earth's a thief,
> That feeds and breeds by a composture stolen
> From general excrement; each thing's a thief.
>   (*Timon of Athens* 4.3)

Kinbote's version, which he hopes "sufficiently approximates the text, or is at least faithful to its spirit," reads thus:

> The sun is a thief: she lures the sea
> and robs it. The moon is a thief:
> he steals his silvery light from the sun.
> The sea is a thief: it dissolves the moon.

Aside from the simple confusion of the gender of sun and moon (a confusion that is appropriate to the translator's personality), several features of Kinbote's translation should be noted. For example, Kinbote's lines emphasize the idea of closedness and circularity, through the omission of the further reference to the earth: the sun steals from the sea, the moon from the sun, the sea from the moon. Certainly Kinbote cannot be expected to endorse Shakespeare's point of the universality of the thievery, since he does not seem conscious of his own complicity in that thievery.

A more noticeable aspect of Kinbote's lines, of course, is the omission of the salient phrase "pale fire", for which the curious reader must check his own copy of *Timon of Athens*, thereby once again doing his part in creating the novel's meaning. But the absence of the crucial phrase only calls our attention to it and to the metaphoric context from which it comes. "[S]ilvery light" is simply a lesser poet's weaker version of the master poet's "pale fire." Nabokov borrowed the line from Shakespeare and lent it to Shade, who actually left it out of his finished poem. Kinbote takes the liberty of using the phrase, which he finds in a rejected line, as the title of Shade's poem.

Whatever his reason, we must agree that Kinbote's decision is an appropriate one. In Shakespeare the phrase is set within the metaphor of cosmic thievery, a notion of which *Pale Fire* itself is an illustration: nature is a great chain of mutual dependencies, a play of lights and borrowed lights—but so is art. The title indirectly reinforces the mysterious dependency of Shade and Kinbote, and even extends it to include Nabokov and Shakespeare. Everyone, including the reader, is caught up in the game of creative thievery.

Kinbote's narrative is not just a madman's ravings, but a comic-romantic siren song that strives to lure its own private truth from Shade's poem. But the effect is mutual. His narrative illuminates and shadows, is illuminated and shadowed by, Shade's poem.

....

7

Space, Time, and Beyond: Ada *and* Transparent Things

Lolita made Nabokov famous and gave him the resources that allowed him to devote himself full time to
writing, that is, to exploring his own consciousness. As a
result, his fiction has become (with the notable exception of
Pnin) increasingly private, though no less interesting. The
demands on the reader's participation, enlarged so greatly
by *Pale Fire*, are just as great in his two most recent
English novels. It is for this reason that the critic Alfred
Kazin has proclaimed that "*Ada* cannot be confidently
explained *in toto* even after several readings," and that
the experience of reading the book is best described as
"travelling and floundering in the mind of that American
genius, Vladimir Vladimirovich Nabokov."[1] The remark
might well be extended to include *Transparent Things*.

Although it is premature to conclude that no further
novels will come from Nabokov's pen, at least one
reviewer has said that in his latest published book, *A Russian Beauty, and Other Stories* (1973), Nabokov seemed
to be tidying up his canon.[2] In addition, the most
recently published interview with Nabokov (1970) reveals
that his current project then was not a new novel, but
an illustrated work on butterflies in art "from Egyptian
antiquity to the Renaissance."[3] Even if they are not his
last novels, we can understand *Ada* and *Transparent
Things* much better, I think, if we recognize that they
are Nabokov's novels about last things. In spite of his
frequently expressed anti-ideological bias, they have, in
other words, a distinctly metaphysical and even eschato-
logical flavor. *Ada* is Nabokov's fullest celebration of the
powers of consciousness, and *Transparent Things* is his
dramatization of the state of consciousness that lies
beyond life.

The privateness of these novels makes them difficult
for the uninitiated, but the lover of his earlier fiction will
rejoice in them. These novels belong together in any

discussion of Nabokov's work, not merely because they come together in point of time, but also because they represent a change in Nabokov's attitude toward his fictional material. After forty years of writing about characters bound and limited by chance, fate, and other villains, he wrote at last about freedom. Not, of course, about absolute or certain freedom, since nothing is absolute or certain in Nabokov's world. Yet one cannot help noticing the weakening of those old tyrants, irony and his companion, parody, and that this weakening makes way for a richer humanity to enter. Nabokov seemed free at last to indulge in his favorite speculations, which are embodied in the myths he created in *Ada* and *Transparent Things*. There is a tentative optimism about these works, so that no matter what Nabokov may yet write, they comprise a moving coda to the harsher music of his earlier fiction.

Ada, or Ardor: A Family Chronicle is an extraordinarily luxuriant piece of fiction stretching to nearly six hundred pages. It is both a myth of love and a romance of mind. Simply put, *Ada* is a memoir written by Van Veen when he is in his nineties, memorializing his love for Ada. But one does not read far before realizing that this particular love affair generates more passionate intensity than that in any of Nabokov's previous stories. At the beginning the affair, which begins when Van is fourteen and Ada, twelve seems normal enough. (At least as compared with Humbert Humbert's nympholepsy or Charles Kinbote's homosexuality.) But Nabokov gradually reveals to the reader (the lovers find out early in their relationship) that their love violates the most serious sexual taboo: incest. Though their parents had managed to conceal the fact from general knowledge, Van is actually Ada's half brother. Yet, as a middle-aged Van later explains to his father, who is at the time trying to break up the affair: "She was twelve . . . and I was a male primatal of fourteen and a half, and we just did not care. And it's too late to care now."

As in *Lolita*, a similar but even higher miracle of art occurs in *Ada*, for Nabokov makes the reader forego his repugnance toward incest and "not care" also. How Nabokov manages this feat is one of the book's most interesting aspects.

The simplest way in which Nabokov mitigates, in relative terms, the "sin" of the lovers is by pointing up the irony in their parents' efforts to keep them moral. After all, the lovers are so closely related precisely because their parents had once played a game of musical beds. Ada was the licit daughter of Dan Veen and Marina Veen. But Van, who was supposed to be the son of Demon Veen (Dan's brother) and Aqua Veen (Marina's sister), is really the illicit offspring of Demon and Marina. To hide the scandal, Demon and Marina took advantage of one of the intermittently mad Aqua's less lucid moments to switch baby Van for Aqua's stillborn child. The children's guilt is thus a guilt passed on from their parents.

A far more important way in which Nabokov softens the guilt is by idealizing the love story, so that the reader feels he is engaged with a myth rather than a social reality. The clinical phrase "male primatal" that Van uses in reference to himself should not be registered as cold objectivity, except insofar as he is trying to minimize emotion in what is obviously a difficult conversation. Instead, the phrase emphasizes, somewhat in the manner of some of Adam Krug's remarks, the primal animal force behind Van's passion. Van, however, is a super-Krug. Krug had merely mortal appetites; but Van Veen is a sexual athlete.

Van is much closer to Krug's biblical namesake, Adam, than Krug is. His affair with Ada begins on her family's estate, at paradisal Ardis Hall. Ada, to whom Nabokov assigned his own hobby of natural history, spends some of her leisure hours (she and Van have nothing else) collecting larvae, manually mating caterpillars, and dreaming of someday founding "a special Institute of Fritillary larvae and violets—all the special violets they breed on." But she also, as his Eve, spends others on nature games with Van that are the foreplay of their lovemaking and on lecturing him on her opinion as to the species of the Tree of Knowledge in the Garden of Eden.

What Nabokov intended by this Edenic imagery we can best learn by collating the novel with ideas found in *Speak, Memory*, where he allowed himself from time to time to talk about his personal beliefs. One helpful passage from the autobiography is the following:

There is . . . keen pleasure (and, after all, what else should the pursuit of science produce?) in meeting the riddle of the initial blossoming of man's mind by postulating a voluptuous pause in the growth of the rest of nature, a lolling and loafing, which allowed first of all the formation of *Homo poeticus*—without which *sapiens* could not have been evolved. "Struggle for life" indeed! The curse of battle and toil leads man back to the boar, to the grunting beast's crazy obsession with the search for food. . . . Toilers of the world, disband! Old books are wrong. The world was made on a Sunday.

Couched in his famous high style are Nabokov's refutations of the two best-known creation myths: the one from Genesis and the one from Darwin. The biblical story represents creation as a labor carried out on six days by God, who then rested on the seventh. Darwin's theory of evolution challenged the biblical myth with the notion that man developed from the lower animals by a process of natural selection in which the fittest survived in the struggle for life. According to Nabokov, both stories are wrong on several counts, but primarily—as he suggested here—because they identify the blossoming of man's mind with work, struggle, and action. In Nabokov's view, the first stage in the development of mind was poetic awareness. Consciousness is the primal quality of man, not rationality or brute force. He even managed to work in a thrust at communism by inserting a parody of the communist slogan, "Workers of the world, unite!" Struggle, toil, and work are not the most natural human states, but the state of conscious awareness.

Joyce Carol Oates was in a sense right when she said that in *Ada* Nabokov focuses "his imagination on the happy few"; but the point is that the few (happy only in Nabokov's special sense) in this case are Nabokov's primal man and woman. What he offers in *Ada* is his private myth of the beginnings of man. *Ada* is not really so much *a* family chronicle as *the* family chronicle. To be sure, the novel has all the usual appurtenances one customarily expects of a family chronicle: a broad range of characters, a sense of historical and geographical background, a plot of sorts covering an extended period of time. There are other touches of ordinariness in the book. In spite of his wealth, Van Veen has a vocation. Again like Adam Krug, he is a philosopher. His success in the field is to be measured by the fact that at the age of thirty-five he is elected to the Rattner Chair of Philosophy at the University of Kingston.

Unlike Krug, however, Van's real talent, as he learns through experience, is not thinking but writing. He is not really *Homo sapiens*, but *Homo poeticus*. This difference accounts in part for the mood of optimism in *Ada*. Having treated Adam Krug like a mere puppet, turning him mad to relieve him of his misery, Nabokov allows the sheer power of Van Veen's artistic genius to sustain him over at least ninety-seven years of life by feeding on his love for Ada.

As with earlier Nabokov characters, uniqueness is the basis both of Van and Ada's lives and of their art (we must note that, though the novel is largely Van's work, Ada is a sometime collaborator; her additions are clearly indicated in the text). But Nabokov gave these characters a supreme uniqueness by giving them his own view of the world and of life, a view that is an amalgam of the artist's presumption (largely from Van) and the joy in biological uniqueness (largely from Ada). One of Ada's most striking contributions is her "scientific" description of the specialness of their affair. Taking "one fairly recent decade" as an example, Ada argues that there must have been "a billion of Bills, good, gifted, tender and passionate, not only spiritually but physically well-meaning Billions," who have "bared the jillions of their no less tender and brilliant Jills."

What makes the case of Ada and Van different is, Ada writes, "the little matter of prodigious individual awareness and young genius, which makes . . . of this or that particular gasp an *unprecedented and unrepeatable* event in the continuum of life." What Ada and Van possess is "that precision of senses and sense" that "must seem unpleasantly peculiar to peasants." Through their genius, these lovers experience not just thrills, but the most highly possible articulated thrills; for them "the detail is all." They are "a unique super-imperial couple."

In Nabokov's myth, as in the biblical, there is also a Fall. Its effects, however, are limited, for, by virtue of their creator's grace, Van and Ada's affair escapes the morbid rabidity that tends to distort love in the earlier fiction. The closest approach to it comes when, after a separation of four years (from the summer of 1884 to the summer of 1888), jealous Van sets out to kill the two

lovers Ada has had in his absence, Percy de Prey and
Monsieur Rack. Van's plan for revenge fizzles. First, he is
wounded by Prey in a duel and must be hospitalized.
Then fate seems to provide him with a chance to salve his
wounded ego, as well as his body, when he learns that
Monsieur Rack is also a patient in the hospital. Rack,
however, dies before Van can put his murder plan into
effect and Percy de Prey, he learns later, has died somewhere on a battlefield.

Although at the time Ada had urged him to forget
those other affairs, Van's plan for murder reveals that at
eighteen he could not quite believe in the uniqueness of
their passion. But after recounting the frustration of his
revenge, he offers a description of their love that is the
artist's echo of Ada's earlier "scientific" description:

What, then, was it that raised the animal act to a level higher
than even that of the most exact arts or the wildest flights of
pure science? It would not be sufficient to say that in his
love-making with Ada he discovered the pang, the *ogon'*, the
agony of supreme "reality." Reality, better say, lost the
quotes it wore like claws—in a world where independent
and original minds must cling to things or pull things apart
in order to ward off madness or death (which is the master
madness). For one spasm or two, he was safe. The new
naked reality needed no tentacle or anchor; it lasted a
moment, but could be repeated as often as he and she were
physically able to make love. The color and fire of that
instant reality depended solely on Ada's identity as perceived
by him.

The frustration of Van's urge for revenge, which
comes at the close of the novel's long Part One, has the
effect of making Van seek some other outlet for his emotion, for he is still separated from Ada. He discovers, as
he says, that he is "pregnant," turns to the writing of
fiction, and publishes *Letters from Terra*, "a philosophical

novel." In Christian mythology, the Fall is redeemed by
the coming of the Son. In Nabokov's myth, the effects of
the Fall are overcome by Van's turning artist. Love and
art keep Van and Ada (or "Vaniada," as they sometimes
refer to themselves to express their physical and spiritual
unity) sane; for to them, love and art, as records of
supreme tenderness, are actually the same thing. The
exercise of sensuous and sensual pleasure is, in fact, the
basis of what one might call (though they do not, nor
does Nabokov) their religion of art and love.

Through Ada and Van, Nabokov introduced into the
story a difficult, but generally comprehensible, view of
history that is intended to contrast Vaniada's beliefs with
those of most of the world. Early in the novel, the insane
Aqua Veen is described, in a confusingly abstract explanation, as a victim of the state of affairs in the 1860s:

Aqua was not quite twenty when the exaltation of her nature
had begun to reveal a morbid trend. Chronologically, the
initial stage of her mental illness coincided with the first
decade of the Great Revelation, and although she might have
found just as easily another theme for her delusion, statistics
shows that the Great, and to some Intolerable, Revelation
caused more insanity in the world than even an over-
preoccupation with religion had in medieval times.

Revelation can be more perilous than Revolution. Sick
minds identified the notion of a Terra planet with that of
another world and this "Other World" got confused not only
with the "Next World" but with the Real World in us and
beyond us. *Our* enchanters, *our* demons, are noble iridescent
creatures with translucent talons and mightily beating wings;
but in the eighteen-sixties the New Believers urged one to
imagine a sphere where our splendid friends had been utterly
degraded, had become nothing but vicious monsters, disgust-
ing devils, with the black scrota of carnivora and the fangs
of serpents, revilers and tormentors of female souls; while

on the opposite side of the cosmic lane a rainbow mist of angelic spirits, inhabitants of sweet Terra, restored all the stalest but still potent myths of old creeds, with rearrangement for melodeon of all the cacophonies of all the divinities and divines ever spawned in the marshes of this our sufficient world.

Although it is by no means easy to guess precisely to what historical events of the 1860s Nabokov attributed the state of affairs described above, one of whose victims was Aqua Veen, we can nevertheless understand in general terms what he and his characters are rejecting. The Great Revelation is a nineteenth-century resurgence of the venerable idea that there exist two worlds, the mundane world of ordinary human experience and the superior divine world to which humans have aspired and which they have envisioned throughout the ages in various forms (the Greek Elysian fields, the Norse Valhalla, the Christian heaven). In *Ada*, the superior divine world is Terra and the ordinary world of human limitations and failings is Anti-Terra or Demonia.

Accompanying this duality in the popular mind is another that Van and Ada also reject. This is the notion of the division of body and soul, and the consequent idea that Terra is a world of purely spiritual bliss, a bliss foreign and unrelated to the purely sensuous and sensual bliss that man can experience through the body on Anti-Terra. It is the belief in these dualities, according to Van and Ada, that drive men mad and lead to death, the ultimate madness.

Having observed the power of this dualistic faith, especially as it affected his supposed mother, Aqua, Van Veen began in his youth to study the phenomenon. His unfinished thesis, based on interviews with "numerous neurotics, among whom there were variety artists, and literary men, and at least three intellectually lucid, but spiritually 'lost' cosmologists," was called "Terra: Eremitic Reality or Collective Dream?" His election to the Rattner Chair of Philosophy was a recognition that he was one of the world's leading Terralogists.

Van is not a believer in Terra (or heaven) as existing apart from the world of sensuous experience. Instead, as early as the age of eighteen, he had begun to believe that Terra was a state of mind achieved through love and art and that he and Ada were "two secret agents in an alien country" or, as Ada put it, "[s]pies from Terra." His philosophical novel, *Letters from Terra*, is written just after he lives through the anguish of jealousy over Ada's other affairs and comes to a fuller understanding of his own idea of heaven, that it is in and through the aesthetic bliss of love and art that one gets one's only glimpses of that realm.

Van and Ada, like Nabokov himself, are philosophical monists, willing to accept heaven only as a mental state achieved through sensuous joy. In that state the world appears as a unity and human experience as harmonious. Like those whom he had interviewed, Van is himself a variety artist (he is a stunt man), a literary artist, and a cosmologist—but not a "lost" one. The power of consciousness, which makes Van and Ada a "super-imperial couple" and artists as well, is the basis of their faith.

Just as Nabokov had earlier made "Ping-pong" Pnin a hero whose jaunty and elemental vitality defied the merely physical laws of Newton, Nabokov gave Van Veen a similar vitality. From early youth Van expressed his defiance of spatial law by walking on his hands. During his college years, he enlivened his leisure hours as a stunt man, performing under the stage name "Mascodagama," which, by its closeness to the name of the Portuguese explorer Vasco da Gama, suggests that Van, too, is a kind

of pioneer. Van's interpretation of the purpose and effect
of maniambulation touches the center of the novel:

It was a standing of metaphor on its head, not for the sake
of the trick's difficulty, but in order to perceive an ascending
waterfall or a sunrise in reverse: a triumph in a sense over
the ardis [arrow] of time. . . . Van on the stage was performing organically what his figures of speech were to perform
later in life—acrobatic wonders that had never been expected
from them and which frightened children.

The stunt is Van's physical defiance of space and
time, not for the sake of defiance but for the sake of a
new and miraculous perspective. It is precisely this perspective that he achieves through his love for Ada and
through his art—that is, through articulated organic
thrills and articulated verbal ones. Once again a gloss
from *Speak, Memory* helps to explain how Van (and
Nabokov himself) conquers time as a writer:

. . . all poetry is positional: to try to express one's position
in regard to the universe embraced by consciousness is an
immemorial urge. The arms of consciousness reach out and
grope, and the longer they are the better. Tentacles, not
wings, are Apollo's natural members. . . . while the scientist
sees everything that happens in one point of space, the poet
feels everything that happens in one point of time. Lost in
thought, he taps his knee with his wandlike pencil, and at
the same instant a car (New York license plate) passes along
the road, a child bangs the screen door of a neighboring
porch, an old man yawns in a misty Turkestan orchard, a
granule of cinder-gray sand is rolled by the wind on Venus,
a Docteur Jacques Hirsch in Grenoble puts on his reading
glasses, and trillions of other such trifles occur—all forming
an instantaneous and transparent organism of events, of
which the poet (sitting in a lawn chair, at Ithaca, N. Y.) is
the nucleus.

Through this power, which Nabokov calls "cosmic synchronization," the poet conquers space and time.

Ada is divided into five parts. The first, comprising just over half of the novel's pages, lavishly chronicles the early stages of Van and Ada's affair, in particular, their first summer together in 1884 and their love's second and more turbulent stage in the summer of 1888. It ends with Van in New York, involved in a passing affair with one of Ada's former school companions, recuperating from the wound he received in the duel with Percy de Prey, and gestating his first novel.

Part Two describes a brief reunion of Van and Ada in 1892, a scheme thought up by a servant at Ardis Hall to blackmail the lovers with pictures he had taken of their lovemaking, and Demon Veen's efforts to break up the affair. Part Three tells of Van's academic career, of Ada's marriage to Andrey Vinelander, and of the suicide of their sister Lucette (like Ada, daughter of Dan and Marina Veen), who was also in love with Van. It ends with the death of Vinelander and the reunion of Van and Ada. Part Four is a summary of Van's most important philosophical treatise, *The Texture of Time* (1924), which is as much poetry as philosophy. In Part Five we find Ada and Van, who have apparently lived joyously together since the death of her husband forty-five years before, celebrating Van's ninety-seventh birthday.

The novel gives the reader a feeling of pure dynamism, a fluid formal movement. This is indeed what Nabokov intended. This reaching toward infinity is what Van means when he says late in the book, "if our . . . couple ever intended to die they would die as it were, *into* the finished book." The reader with the perseverance to finish it will find, in fact, that *Ada* does not really end at all, but spirals back into itself: the last few paragraphs are a summary of its charms of plot and descriptive detail that sounds like a blurb for the dust jacket.

Just as *Letters from Terra* was Van Veen's "first philosophical novel," *Ada* is Nabokov's, but it is not his last, for *Transparent Things* constitutes part two of Nabokov's fictional statement of belief. On the surface, the differences between the two works could hardly be greater. *Transparent Things* is as deliberately limited in length (a mere one hundred pages) as *Ada* is spun out. Whereas Van Veen is Nabokov's superhero because he is successful in enjoying a seemingly endless life of art and love, Hugh Person, the principal character in the later novel (whose name is meant to sound like "You Person"), is almost completely lacking in distinction. Having exhaustively painted in words the life story of a genius of supreme achievement, Nabokov turned to describe the genius *manqué*, one of Ada's sensitive "billions of Bills" who does not succeed in self-fulfillment.

Yet Nabokov is generous to Hugh Person in death as he was to Van Veen in life. *Ada* is the record of lovers who achieve a kind of immortality, a triumph over space and time through art and love. *Transparent Things* is a novel about death, but a very unusual one: it is narrated from the perspective of the other side of death. As *Ada* makes clear, that other side cannot be justly represented by any of the ordinary conceptions, such as heaven; but *Transparent Things* leaves no doubt that the other side exists.

At the age of forty, the colorless and unaggressive Hugh Person revisits Switzerland, the scene of several crucial events in his life. On his first visit there, at twenty-two, he had accompanied his father, an American businessman. Hugh's strongest feelings about his father were mute annoyance and embarrassment at his father's growing clumsiness. The middle-aged father's sudden death, a bit of grotesquery that took place in a dressing room of a clothing store, was, instead of traumatic, only mildly troublesome to Hugh, who thought that he must "do something about a number of recollected unkindnesses of which he had been guilty up to that very day."

Hugh cleared his conscience by following the advice, received by telephone, of "an uncle in Scranton" and having his father's body promptly cremated, thus getting "rid of the dreadful object practically at once." What he then experienced was the "sense of liberation . . . a great breeze, ecstatic and clean, blowing away a lot of life's rot." One stimulus of this feeling of liberation was his delight in finding three thousand dollars in his father's wallet. Without knowing anything about his father's financial affairs, Hugh mistakenly viewed the money as a promise of a large inheritance.

In comparison with Van Veen, whose experience in life reaches the limits of fullness and luxuriance, Hugh Person appears as an underprivileged (in Nabokov's view a merely average) character, whose lot is one of spiritual shallowness, "the lot of brilliant young people who lack any special gift or ambition and get accustomed to applying only a small part of their wits to humdrum or charlatan tasks." In the ten years following his father's death, Hugh wandered from project to project, job to job. His literary pretensions resulted in his publishing a poem in a college magazine and a letter in the London *Times*, and in his serving for seven years as the secretary to "a notorious fraud, the late symbolist Atman." Moving for a time to the stationery business, he accomplished his greatest achievement: he invented "The Person Pen," presumably an improved fountain pen. He ended up at twenty-nine working for a publishing firm, by which time he had settled into being a "sulky person," a "sullen slave."

Hugh's love life reveals his greatest poverty. A virgin when his father died, his initial act of freedom was to accost the first prostitute he could find and lose his virginity. Previously he had unsuccessfully courted a mother and then her daughter, and even the prostitute brutally berated him as "a poor performer." When at thirty-two he returned to Switzerland on business, to deal with a touchy client, a writer for his firm, he met—by a means Nabokov calls "ideally banal"—Armande, an attractive but cold woman, whom he eventually married and murdered one night while in a trancelike state. After his trial and years in an asylum, Hugh returned again to Switzerland, haunted now by the deaths of both his father and his wife. There, trying nostalgically to recapture a vision of his wife (whom he really loved), Hugh himself dies.

Hugh's spiritual banality does not limit the novel's interest, for that interest lies much less in the characters than in the narrative technique. In *Transparent Things* Nabokov employed a chatty narrative style. But more than that, it is as if the story were being told not by an individual at all but by a crowd. One might, of course, assume that Nabokov is speaking in the royal plural, when he says (as in the beginning of chapter seventeen), "We shall now discuss love," or (as in chapter nineteen) "We are back in New York and this is their last evening together." Or one might argue, particularly of the latter quotation, that Nabokov used the plural to approximate a tone of cozy informality in order to include the reader in the pursuit of Hugh. Since chapter twenty-one is a letter from the pen of R, the author whom Hugh had visited, and since R's style has the same chattiness as that of the novel's narrator, some readers have seen in *Trans-*

parent Things a narrative game like that of *Pale Fire* and have identified R as "the unseen author of the book."[4]

Yet such speculations simply cannot account for passages such as the one in which the narrator speaks about his relation to Hugh:

Direct interference in a person's life does not enter our scope of activity, nor, on the other . . . hand, is his destiny a chain of predeterminate links: some "future" events may be likelier than others, O. K., but all are chimeric. . . .

Only chaos would result if some of us championed Mr. X, while another group backed Miss Julia Moore. . . . The most we can do when steering a favorite in the best direction, in circumstances not involving injury to others, is to act as a breath of wind and to apply the lightest, the most indirect pressure. . . .

The narrative technique Nabokov used here is intelligible only if *Transparent Things* is considered in the context of Nabokov's entire canon. The best clue to the novel as a whole comes from *Pnin*:

Pnin slowly walked under the solemn pines. The sky was dying. He did not believe in an autocratic God. He did believe, dimly, in a democracy of ghosts. The souls of the dead, perhaps, formed committees, and there, in continuous session, attended to the destinies of the quick.

In *Transparent Things* Nabokov adopted the point of view of the ghosts who watch over Hugh Person (and whose company Hugh joins at the novel's end), urging him gently in one direction or another, urging gently because even here Nabokov avoided absolutes. The novel is tentatively optimistic about the life that comes after death, a life that Nabokov described with equal tentativeness in *Speak, Memory*:

. . . every dimension presupposes a medium within which it can act, and if, in the spiral unwinding of things, space warps into something akin to time, and time, in its turn, warps into something akin to thought, then surely, another dimension follows—a special Space, not the old one, we trust, unless spirals become vicious circles again.

Like all his other novels, *Transparent Things* is essentially a commentary on "the game of worlds"; but this one has an air of poignant finality about it, for this time the commentary is offered by those who run the show from their "special Space" beyond space, time, and thought.

Notes

Introduction

1. For Brown's remark, see his review of the Russian translation of *Lolita, New Republic*, 20 January 1968, p. 20. Leonard's remark is the title of his review of *Ada*; see *The New York Times*, 1 May 1969, p. 45.
2. *Washington Post Book Week*, 26 September 1965, pp. 2–3.
3. Herbert Gold, "The Art of Fiction XL: Vladimir Nabokov, An Interview," *The Paris Review* 41 (1967): 111.
4. Ibid., p. 100.
5. Ibid.
6. Ibid., p. 111.
7. "Inspiration," *The Saturday Review of the Arts* 1, no. 1 (6 January 1973) :30–32.
8. Gold, "The Art of Fiction," p. 96.
9. Alfred Appel, Jr., "An Interview with Vladimir Nabokov," in *Nabokov: The Man and His Work*, ed. L. S. Dembo (Madison: University of Wisconsin Press, 1967), pp. 24–25.
10. Ibid., p. 21.
11. For a brief survey of the controversy caused by Nabokov's translation of *Eugene Onegin*, see Clarence

Brown, "Nabokov's Pushkin and Nabokov's Nabokov," in *Nabokov: The Man and His Work*, ed. L. S. Dembo, pp. 195–96.

12. Ibid., p. 207.
13. I am condensing here Auden's remarks from his "Introduction," in *Romantic Poets* (New York: Modern Library, n. d.), pp. xii–xxvi.
14. Gold, "The Art of Fiction," pp. 95–96.
15. Appel, "An Interview," p. 130.
16. "A Personal View of Nabokov," *The Saturday Review of the Arts* 1, no. 1 (6 January 1973) :37.

1.   Roots of Remembered Greenery

1. R. H. W. Dillard, "Not Text, But Texture: The Novels of Vladimir Nabokov," in *The Sounder Few* ed. R. H. W. Dillard, George Garrett, and John Rees Moore (Athens, Ga.: University of Georgia Press, 1971), p. 141.
2. Alfred Appel, Jr., "Conversations with Nabokov," *Novel* 4 (1970–71) :211.
3. Robert C. Williams, "Memory's Defense: The Real Life of Vladimir Nabokov's Berlin," *The Yale Review* 60 (1970–71) :242–43.
4. For example, Ross Wetzsteon, "Nabokov as Teacher," *TriQuarterly* 17 (Winter 1970) :240–46.
5. Ibid., p. 241.
6. Morris Bishop, "Nabokov at Cornell," *TriQuarterly*, p. 239.
7. Appel, "Conversations," p. 209.
8. Ibid., p. 215.

2.   The Gloom and the Glory of Exile:
The Russian Novels

1. Granville Hicks, "The Birth of a Bard," *Saturday Review*, 1 June 1963, p. 48.
2. R. H. W. Dillard, "Not Text, But Texture: The Novels

of Vladimir Nabokov," in *The Sounder Few*, ed.
R. H. W. Dillard, George Garrett, and John Rees Moore
(Athens, Ga.: University of Georgia Press, 1971), p.
141.

3. Gleb Struve, "Notes on Nabokov as a Russian Writer,"
in *Nabokov: The Man and His Work*, ed. L. S. Dembo
(Madison: University of Wisconsin Press, 1967), p. 46.

4. Gleb Struve, "Russian Literature," in *Encyclopedia of
World Literature in the Twentieth Century*, ed. Wolf-
gang Bernard Fleischmann, 3 vols. (New York: Frederick Ungar Publishing Co., 1967–71), 3:205.

5. Andrew Field, *Nabokov, His Life in Art* (Boston: Little,
Brown, and Co., 1967), pp. 9–10.

6. Clarence Brown, "Nabokov's Pushkin and Nabokov's
Nabokov," in *Nabokov: The Man and His Work*, ed.
L. S. Dembo, p. 200.

7. Herbert Gold, "The Art of Fiction XL: Vladimir
Nabokov, An Interview," *Paris Review* 41 (Summer–
Fall 1967):97.

8. Field, *Nabokov*, p. 153; Charles Nicol, "Nabokov's
Card Trick," *Atlantic Monthly*, June 1968, p. 108.

9. In one of the most recent interviews, Nabokov has given
information about his interest in films. *See* Alfred
Appel, Jr., "Conversations with Nabokov," *Novel* 4
(1970–71):211–15.

10. Field, *Nabokov*, p. 160; Dabney Stuart, "*Laughter in
the Dark*: Dimensions of Parody," *TriQuarterly* 17
(Winter 1970):72–95.

11. Field, *Nabokov*, p. 117.

12. *See*, for example, Field, *Nabokov*, pp. 117–18.

13. Appel, "Conversations," p. 209.

3. *Fables of Genius:*
The Real Life of Sebastian Knight *and* Bend Sinister

1. *See* Andrew Field, *Nabokov, His Life in Art* (Boston:
Little, Brown, and Co., 1967), p. 26.

2. Alfred Appel, Jr., "An Interview with Vladimir Nabokov," in *Nabokov: The Man and His Work*, ed. L. S. Dembo (Madison: University of Wisconsin Press, 1967), p. 33.

4. *Aesthetic Bliss:* Lolita

1. For these and other examples, *see Nabokov: The Man and His Work*, ed. L. S. Dembo (Madison: University of Wisconsin Press, 1967), pp. 247–52.
2. Lionel Trilling, "The Last Lover: Vladimir Nabokov's *Lolita*," *Encounter* 11 (October 1958):15.
3. For background on the sonnet, see Maurice Valency, *In Praise of Love: An Introduction to the Love-Poetry of the Renaissance* (New York: Macmillan, 1958).
4. Trilling, "The Last Lover," p. 17.
5. Ernest Becker, "Everyman as Pervert," *Angel in Armor: A Post-Freudian Perspective on the Nature of Man* (New York: George Braziller, 1969), pp. 1–38.
6. Becker explicitly denies this connection (*see* p. 11 of his essay), but his demur may not hold in the case of Humbert Humbert.
7. Becker, "Everyman as Pervert," p. 15.
8. Ibid., pp. 16–17.
9. Alfred Appel, Jr., "An Interview with Vladimir Nabokov," in *Nabokov: The Man and His Work*, ed. L. S. Dembo, p. 31.
10. Ibid., p. 39.
11. Though the postscript did not appear in the first edition and was added later, Nabokov has subsequently included it in all further editions and in the many translations. He seems to consider it now an integral part of the text, like the foreword by the fictitious John Ray.

6.   *A Game of Worlds:*   Pale Fire

1. Mary McCarthy, "Vladimir Nabokov's *Pale Fire*," *Encounter* 19 (October 1962) :71.
2. Andrew Field's remark that the title of the novel has "absolutely no relevance whatsoever to Shade's poem taken by itself" seems to me quite wrong-headed. *See* Field, *Nabokov, His Life in Art* (Boston: Little, Brown, and Co., 1967), p. 298.

7.   *Space, Time, and Beyond:*
Ada *and* Transparent Things

1. "In the Mind of Nabokov," *The Saturday Review*, 10 May 1969, p. 27.
2. *See* Paul Zweig's review of *A Russian Beauty and Other Stories*, *New York Review of Books*, 29 April 1973, p. 21.
3. Alfred Appel, Jr., "Conversations with Nabokov," *Novel* 4 (1970–71) :216.
4. *See* the review by Michael Wood, "Tender Trousers," *New York Review of Books*, 16 November 1972, p. 12.

Bibliography

1. Works by Vladimir Nabokov

Ada, or Ardor: A Family Chronicle. New York: McGraw-Hill Book Co., 1969.

Bend Sinister. New York: H. Holt, 1947. Republished in a *Time* Reading Program Special Edition, with an introduction by the author. New York: Time, Inc., 1964.

Camera obscura. London: J. Long, 1936. Substantially altered version, titled *Laughter in the Dark*, Indianapolis and New York: The Bobbs-Merrill Co., 1938.

The Defense. New York: G. P. Putnam's, 1964.

Despair. London: J. Long, 1937. Revised edition, New York: G. P. Putnam's, 1966.

Eugene Onegin: A Novel in Verse (by Alexander Pushkin). Translation from the Russian, with a commentary by Vladimir Nabokov. 4 vols. New York: Pantheon Books, 1964.

The Eye. New York: Phaedra, 1965.

The Gift. New York: G. P. Putnam's, 1963.

Glory. New York: McGraw-Hill Book Co., 1971.

Invitation to a Beheading. New York: G. P. Putnam's, 1959.

King, Queen, Knave. New York: McGraw-Hill Book Co., 1968.

Lolita. 2 vols. Paris: Olympia Press, 1955. American edition, New York: G. P. Putnam's, 1958.

Mary. New York: McGraw-Hill Book Co., 1970.

Nabokov's Dozen: A Collection of Thirteen Stories. Garden City, N. Y.: Doubleday, 1958.

Nikolai Gogol. Norfolk, Conn.: New Directions, 1944. Corrected edition, New York: A New Directions Paperbook, 1961.

Camera obscura. London: J. Long, 1936. Substantially altered version, titled *Laughter in the Dark,* Indianapolis and New York: The Bobbs-Merrill Co., 1938.

Nine Stories. Norfolk, Conn.: New Directions, 1947.

Pale Fire. New York: G. P. Putnam's, 1962.

Pnin. Garden City, N. Y.: Doubleday, 1957.

Poems. New York: Doubleday, 1959.

Poems and Problems. New York: McGraw-Hill Book Co., 1970.

Quartet. New York: Phaedra, 1966. Under title, *Nabokov's Quartet,* London: Weidenfeld and Nicolson, 1967.

The Real Life of Sebastian Knight. Norfolk, Conn.: New Directions, 1941.

A Russian Beauty, and Other Stories. New York: McGraw-Hill Book Co., 1973.

The Song of Igor's Campaign: An Epic of the Twelfth Century. Translation from Old Russian. New York: Vintage Books, 1960.

Speak, Memory: An Autobiography Revisited. New York: G. P. Putnam's, 1966. Original edition titled *Conclusive Evidence,* New York: Harper & Bros., 1951.

Strong Opinions. New York: McGraw-Hill Book Co., 1973.

Three Russian Poets: Selections from Pushkin, Lermontov, and Tyutchev. Translations. Norfolk, Conn.: New Directions, 1944.

Transparent Things. New York: McGraw-Hill Book Co., 1972.

The Waltz Invention. New York: Phaedra, 1966.

2. *Works about Vladimir Nabokov*

Appel, Alfred, Jr. "Conversations with Nabokov." *Novel* 4 (1970–71) :209–22.

———. Introduction to *The Annotated Lolita*, by Vladimir Nabokov. New York: McGraw-Hill Book Co., 1970.

Bader, Julia. *The Crystal Land: Artifice in Nabokov's English Novels*. Berkeley and Los Angeles: University of California Press, 1972.

Bok, Sissela. "Redemption through Art in Nabokov's *Ada*." *Critique* 12, no. 3 (1971) :110–20.

Dembo, L. S., ed. *Nabokov: The Man and His Work*. Madison, Wisc.: University of Wisconsin Press, 1967.

Field, Andrew. *Nabokov, His Life in Art: A Critical Narrative*. Boston: Little, Brown, and Co., 1967.

Gold, Herbert. "The Art of Fiction XL: Vladimir Nabokov, An Interview." *Paris Review* 41 (Summer–Fall 1967) : 92–111.

Green, Martin. "The Morality of *Lolita*." *Kenyon Review* 28 (1966) :352–77.

Josipovici, G. D. "*Lolita:* Parody and the Pursuit of Beauty." *Critical Quarterly* 6 (1964) :35–48.

Lee, L. L. "Vladimir Nabokov's Great Spiral of Being." *Western Humanities Review* 18 (1964) :225–36.

McCarthy, Mary. "Vladimir Nabokov's *Pale Fire*." *Encounter* 19 (October 1962) :71–72, 74, 76–78, 80–82, 84.

Mitchell, Charles. "Mythic Seriousness in *Lolita*." *Texas Studies in Literature and Language* 5 (1963) :329–43.

Nicol, Charles. "Pnin's History." *Novel* 4 (1970–71) :197–208.

Proffer, Carl R. *Keys to "Lolita."* Bloomington, Ind.: University of Indiana Press, 1968.

Pryce-Jones, Alan. "The Fabulist's Worlds: Vladimir Nabokov." In *The Creative Present: Notes on Contemporary American Fiction*. Eds. Nona Balakian and Charles Simmons. Garden City, New York: Doubleday, 1963. Pp. 65–78.

Rowe, William Woodin. *Nabokov's Deceptive World*. New York: New York University Press, 1971.

Schaeffer, Susan Fromberg. "*Bend Sinister* and the Novelist as Anthropomorphic Deity." *Centennial Review* 17 (1973):115–51.

Stegner, Page. *Escape into Aesthetics; The Art of Vladimir Nabokov*. New York: The Dial Press, 1966.

Stuart, Dabney. "*The Real Life of Sebastian Knight*: Angles of Perception," *Modern Language Quarterly* 29 (1968): 312–28.

Trilling, Lionel. "The Last Lover: Vladimir Nabokov's *Lolita*." *Encounter* 11 (October 1958):9–19.

TriQuarterly: For Vladimir Nabokov on His Seventieth Birthday. Edited by Alfred Appel, Jr., and Charles Newman. 17 (Winter 1970).

Williams, Carol T. " 'Web of Sense': *Pale Fire* in the Nabokov Canon." *Critique* 6, no. 3 (1963):29–45.

Williams, Robert C. "Memory's Defense: The Real Life of Vladimir Nabokov's Berlin." *Yale Review* 60 (1970–71):241–50.

Zimmer, Dieter E. *Vladimir Nabokov; Bibliographie des Gesamtwerks*. Reinbek bei Hamburg: Rowohlt, 1963.

Index